wicazō śa review

A Journal of Native American Studies

Editor
James Riding In, Arizona State University

Associate Editors
Amy Lonetree, University of California, Santa Cruz
Nicole Blalock, Arizona State University

Founding Editors
Elizabeth Cook-Lynn
Roger Buffalohead
Beatrice Medicine
William Willard

Contributing Editors
Duane Champagne, University of California, Los Angeles
Steven J. Crum, University of California, Davis
Ellen Cushman, Michigan State University
Clayton Dumont, San Francisco State University
Donald Fixico, Arizona State University
Julia Good Fox, Haskell Indian Nations University
Lawrence Gross, University of Redlands
Joy Harjo, University of California, Los Angeles
Suzan Shown Harjo, The Morning Star Institute
Tom Holm, University of Arizona
Craig Howe, Oglala Lakota College
Ted Jojola, University of New Mexico
Glenabah Martinez, University of New Mexico
Cornel Pewewardy, Portland State University
Lisa Poupart, University of Wisconsin, Green Bay
Kathryn Shanley, University of Montana
Luci Tapahonso, University of New Mexico
Laura Tohe, Arizona State University
Edward Valandra, University of South Dakota, Vermillion
Michael Yellow Bird, Humboldt State University

CONTENTS

Articles

The Divided Yoeme (Yaqui) People

Christina Leza

Yoeme (Yaqui)[1] roots lie in Northern Mexico, in the Yoeme homelands known as the *biakim*. At the turn of the twentieth century, Porfiriato policies for treating the "Indian problem"[2] in Mexico resulted in the Yoeme being subjected to genocidal warfare, deportation to distant southern Mexican plantations, and forced migration north into the United States. Many of the Yoeme who migrated to the United States settled together as communities in southern Arizona. Certain Arizona Yoeme communities who settled permanently in the United States would eventually gain federal recognition as a U.S. tribal nation, the Pascua Yaqui Tribe. This shift in political status from "immigrants from the Mexican state of Sonora"[3] to a U.S. tribal nation ultimately resulted in correlated identity shifts for Arizona Yoeme as Pascua Yaqui lives were transformed by the Western colonial structures of tribal governance, U.S.–Mexico border imperialism, and dominant nationalist and regional ideologies about Mexican citizens as "Other."

Holm, Pearson, and Chavis have proposed a revised version of Robert K. Thomas's peoplehood model as a core theoretical framework for conceptualizing indigenous group identities and indigenous sovereignty.[4] The model is presented as an interconnected matrix of an indigenous people's language, sacred history, land/territory, and ceremonial cycle, in which all four aspects of an indigenous people's identity are intertwined and essential. The model, founded on Edward H. Spicer's conceptualization of the Yoeme as a "persistent people," provides a strong

basis for understanding the survival of certain indigenous group identities through time. It also provides concrete means for conceptualizing indigenous sovereignty outside of the Western nation-state model
of citizenship and governmental power. This essay argues that while
shared language, sacred history, ceremonial structure, and connections
to the hiakim continue to unite Yoeme as a binational people across the
U.S.–Mexico political border, U.S. border enforcement policies and
other colonial mechanisms have created both physical and ideological
schisms within the Yoeme community that threaten the Yoeme binational peoplehood.

The thoughts presented in this essay are based on fieldwork and
interviews with Yoeme political activists and other border indigenous
activists conducted in the Phoenix/Tucson area of Arizona from 2006
to 2012, and draw significantly from ethnographic and life history
interviews with political activist and Yoeme ceremonial leader José
Matus. Matus was asked to serve as a ceremonial leader in his teens and
was told by his elders at the time that he, like other ceremonial leaders, would have the responsibility of protecting and passing on Yoeme
knowledge. Born in 1951, he witnessed the transition of the Arizona
Yoeme community to federal tribal status in 1978. As a ceremonial
leader during this period, Matus was attentive to the community interests and politics that guided this transition and was actively involved
in the recognition process. He considers this period of federal recognition work with other Arizona Yoeme leaders as his training in both
Yoeme advocacy and broader community advocacy. In 2006, Matus
was director of both the Coalición de Derechos Humanos (Human
Rights Coalition) and the Alianza Indígena Sin Fronteras (Indigenous
Alliance Without Borders), both nonprofit border rights organizations.
At that time, Matus was sought out for his expertise on border-crossing
procedures for Sonora Yaqui when entering the United States for tribal
projects. As will be discussed, Matus's knowledge of border policy
and procedure has always been necessarily tied to his role as a ceremonial leader. And his dedication to border rights activism and border
reform are critically tied to his ceremonial responsibility to preserve
and strengthen Yaqui traditional knowledge.

Given Matus's position as a ceremonial leader in the Yoeme community and his critical understanding of Yoeme border-crossing issues,
his voice is a privileged one in this essay. By highlighting this voice, this
essay also aims to bring forward a traditional voice that has been marginalized in public discourse on Yoeme border crossing. During the period of Spanish Jesuit occupancy in the Yoeme homelands, the Yoeme
developed a leadership structure for maintaining traditional authority in balance with newly introduced Western governmental leadership roles through what Spicer referred to as the five Yoeme "realms
of authority."[5] Four of the five realms consist of religious and ceremo-

nial leadership, while one realm is represented by the civil authorities typically recognized by state officials as the governing authorities in Yoeme communities. This five-part leadership structure is a system of "closely interlocked authorities, which may take the lead in certain important matters, but whose decisions are always subject to review by and adjustment with the other authorities."[6] It is a system that has ensured the participation of ceremonial leadership at all levels of local governance for centuries despite the imposition of Western governance structures.[7] Yet, while there is continued respect for ceremonial leadership in Arizona Yoeme communities, the increasing bureaucracy of tribal governance has restricted the ability of ceremonial leadership to participate in tribal decision making. This essay addresses the marginalization of ceremonial authority in decision making using border policy as an example, and brings forward Matus's voice as a ceremonial authority with critical knowledge on issues related to Yoeme border crossing.

Although Matus's voice is privileged in this essay, this should by no means suggest that Matus's perspectives are representative of the Yoeme people. Ultimately, Matus's statements will help illustrate that among Arizona Yoeme there are varied understandings of Yoeme identity, and differing opinions on to what extent cross-border connections are needed to maintain traditional Yoeme lifeways as well as on which issues should be prioritized in tribal government policy and programming. Among Arizona Yoeme we find the kind of ideological heterogeneity that one should expect to find in any contemporary indigenous community embedded within a larger nation-state, including the type of general "progressive" / "traditional" divide that arises in indigenous communities as a result of dominant socioeconomic pressures.[8] By exploring the apparent "progressive" / "traditional" split among Arizona Yaqui in regard to border policy, this essay seeks to illuminate how the U.S.–Mexico border impacts Arizona Yoeme identities and Yoeme transnational relationships.

Border scholar Robert R. Alvarez Jr. observes that even such a monumental work as Spicer's *Cycles of Conquest*, which examines the impact of Spain, Mexico, and the United States on Native peoples of the Southwest over the course of five centuries, "does not consider the political border as a meaningful variable."[9] Despite the recent trend toward transnational culture studies, there has continued to be a general disregard for the effect of international borders when describing cultures overlapping such borders. There has certainly been a glaring absence of U.S.–Mexico border policy discussion in critical scholarship on the Yoeme. Much of the scholarly literature on the Yoeme has focused on the Yoeme as a "persistent people."[10] The Yoeme have been remarkably successful in gaining political recognition as a people in both Mexico and the United States. In Mexico, the Yoeme are the only indigenous people with a federally recognized land reserve created by presidential decree. In the United States, the Yoeme are the only indigenous people once classified as "immigrants" from Mexico to have gained federal recognition as a tribal nation. With some support from the Pascua Yaqui Tribe in Arizona and continued cross-border communication between traditional leadership, Yoeme ceremonial group members, traditional healers, and other Yoeme cultural specialists from the hiakim in the Río Yaqui region of Sonora maintain a presence within the Arizona Yoeme communities today. In the Greater Southwest, the Yoeme certainly stand out for having retained so much of their original territories and their traditional language and customs throughout the periods of Spanish colonialism, the development of the Mexican nation-state, and the forced and widespread diaspora.

There is no doubt that the Yoeme are a persistent people. Yet, a focus on Yoeme political and cultural persistence risks essentializing the Yoeme, whereby persistence is perceived as an essential social trait. It is therefore easy to miss the tremendous identity work done by Yoemes[11] as well as the level of political organization necessary to maintain Yoeme cultural persistence. Given the Yoeme's successful adaptation to and resistance against the various imperial and state policies designed to marginalize Yoeme society, it is also easy to underestimate the extent to which certain contemporary state policies now limit Yoeme sociopolitical organization. At present, the political and ceremonial structures that have secured Yoeme cultural persistence through history are significantly threatened by escalating border enforcement and the limitations of U.S. tribal self-governance. In addition, the challenges faced by the Yoeme are not just a matter of restricted movement between Yoeme communities, but also of how the enforced border impacts Yoeme perceptions of group identity.[12]

As a ceremonial leader, Matus is greatly concerned with the loss of Yoeme language in Arizona Yoeme communities and the difficulties he faces in passing on ceremonial knowledge without being able to communicate this knowledge to Yaqui youth in the traditional language. His fear that one day Yoeme ceremonies will "be a thing of the past," with ceremonial groups performing "like actors going through the [motions] in our community centers," is shaped by his ability to observe the shifts in Yoeme language and culture on both sides of the border. While the number of fluent Yoeme language speakers in Sonora greatly outnumber those found in the United States, it is clear that the future of Yoeme language and ceremonial persistence in the Río Yaqui communities is uncertain as youth rapidly leave rural Sonora Yoeme communities in search of better economic opportunities. Matus states, "[Arizona Yaqui] need the people from Río Yaqui. We need to be able to work with them . . . We're going to lose a lot . . . They're going to lose a lot. We're all at risk now."

José Matus has witnessed many changes in the Arizona Yoeme community. Growing up in Barrio Libre (Free Neighborhood) in the 1950s and 1960s, Matus remembers a large community populated with indigenous peoples including Yoeme and O'odham as well as Chicano families. Construction of a new highway system in the late sixties resulted in eminent domain removal of neighborhood households and a reduced indigenous population within Barrio Libre. Matus and his family remained in the Yaqui community of Barrio Libre, and it is there that Matus would develop into the roles of ceremonial leader and community advocate.

Matus began ceremonial work when he was eight years old. In the Yoeme tradition, individuals are called to serve in a particular ceremonial society through a *manda*, or vow. Children are typically promised to a ceremonial society during a period of extreme illness when parents or guardians seek assistance in curing.[13] Matus was promised to ceremonial service through a vow made by his grandmother. Matus's service would be lifelong, "to thank the Creator for getting well."

At the age of around seventeen, Matus was asked by the ceremonial elders of Barrio Libre to help them in bringing in ceremonial participants from Río Yaqui, Mexico. Matus was very familiar with the Río Yaqui region. Having grown up with his grandmother, he would often go with her to visit with relatives in Potam pueblo (town), where he would stay for weeks and sometimes months. When he was asked by the elders to go to Río Yaqui, Matus says, "My thoughts were with helping my elders bring in people that we needed for ceremonies, and that was my calling and my task and my service to the ceremonial society that I belonged to, and that was something that was required of me. So I just did it." Nevertheless, Matus recalls feeling a bit "intimidated" by this new responsibility that he was being asked to take on as a part of his ceremonial service. "They said, 'We want you to do this. Go get some of the participants in Río Yaqui. We need a deer dancer and we need a violin player, so you go seek them out.' . . . I had never done that before, and I was just wondering, 'How am I going to do that?' . . . That was the biggest responsibility of my life."

Matus describes a "long learning process" involved in taking on this new ceremonial role, which began with his first trip to Río Yaqui to recruit ceremonial participants. Matus was driven to Nogales where he caught a bus to Potam pueblo. Arriving alone in Potam, in the early morning, Matus says that he was not sure where to go from there. He had relatives in Potam and some ideas about where to go, but there would be no transportation until later in the morning. He decided to walk over to a restaurant nearby to have some coffee. While sitting and drinking his coffee he noticed "an elder gentleman" sitting about three or four tables across from him and watching him. Remembering this, Matus says, "That kind of made me nervous, because I didn't know why he was looking at me . . . So, finally I saw him get up and he came over, and he started talking to me . . . Then finally he asked me what I was doing. He knew I wasn't from around there, and he asked me, 'Where are you from?' I told him, 'I'm from Tucson.' And he said, 'Well, what are you doing here? Are you with somebody else? Or are you by yourself?' 'Well, I'm here by myself, and I'm here to get some pascolas[14] and a deer dancer and take them to Tucson,' I said. He said, 'Oh yeah? Who are you going to get?' And I said, 'Well, I don't know yet. I'm not sure who, or where to go, actually.' And he says, 'Well, there's one guy, he's a pascola dancer. He's an elder. He lives right across the street from here. I can take you to him.' . . . So, basically, that's how I was able to recruit people. He took me to this guy, and that guy took me to another guy, and we spent the whole day going around talking to people." Matus asked the elder pascola to speak on his behalf when making contact with the other Río Yaqui ceremonial participants, and through the Río Yaqui elder, began learning the regional formalities for establishing ceremonial relationships between Yoeme communities.

José still faced challenges when crossing the border into the United States with the ten ceremonial participants that were recruited from Río Yaqui:

> That's where the problems began. Number one, the border officials did not want to let them through because they didn't have identification . . . So I talked to the supervisor, and he says, "No. They need to have their passport . . . and they need to go back home until they get their passports." So I said, "Well, is there anyone else I can talk to?" So I talked to the codirector. And the codirector said, "No." So I was telling him, "It's important for us to have these people cross the border for these ceremonies." Then I was explaining to him what they did and what each person's calling was . . . So after a long discussion with them, they took a look and then said, "Okay, this is what we're going to do. We're going to parole them in." And that was something that I'd never heard of, "parole them in," other than they were in prison, and they were let go and paroled after leaving the prison, like they just got out of jail. So I said, "Well, what do you mean 'parole'? They're not coming from prison." He said, "No, no, that's what we call it. 'Parole' them in. That means you're going to have to sign for them . . . we have a form here [saying] that you promise that they'll come back and that they're going to ceremony, and that they'll come back on so and so date but it's going

to cost you ninety dollars per application, per applicant."
And I said, "Well, I don't have nine hundred dollars. I don't
even have a hundred dollars. I just spent all the money getting them down to Nogales on the bus," I said. So, again,
he said, "Well, that's the only way I can do it." So, I started
negotiating with him again. So, he said, "Well, I'll waive
the fee. We'll get 'em through, 'cuz I know you've been
here for a long time waiting to cross the border with your
people. So, we'll just let it go this time, but next time this is
what you need to do."

About a year after that first trip across the border with Río Yaqui
ceremonial participants, the ceremonial elders spoke to Matus about
joining the ceremonial leadership. At the time, Matus believed that he
was too young to take on the responsibilities of a ceremonial leader. So
he spoke with his elders, his mother, and his uncles who also participated in ceremonies and told them that he didn't "want any part of this
large responsibility" because he didn't know if he was "going to be able
to handle it." But they said, "'Well, that's why you have the ceremonial
leaders right now. And that's why they want to start training you, so
that you know what to do. All you have to do is observe, listen and
ask questions, and that way you can learn.' So they did not let me back
out on that. They said, 'They want you. And you're going to stay here
whether you want to or not.' I really didn't have a choice. You know?
So I said, 'Well, fine. I'll do whatever I can.'" Matus accepted his new
calling and entered the ceremonial leadership in his late teens, despite
some trepidation.

Yaqui ceremonial leaders of Barrio Libre began bringing in ceremonial participants from Río Yaqui around the 1930s.[15] This was part
of the process of reconstructing ceremonial life in this small Yaqui community. At this time, Barrio Libre had a deer dancer[16] and a *tampaleo*, but
the Yaqui of Barrio Libre needed additional pascolas and musicians to
hold their traditional ceremonies in what they now saw as their own
pueblo in Arizona. Sustained contact between Yaqui in Sonora and
Arizona and the relative openness of the U.S.–Mexico border in this
early period secured the success of this type of transborder ceremonial organizing. In the late sixties when Matus was given the task of
bringing in ceremonial participants from Mexico, there had been no
dramatic changes to immigration policy impacting border crossing.
By this point, however, the Border Patrol had grown administratively,
and there was increasing attention to border-crossing procedure.
While Matus's role as a devoted Barrio Libre ceremonial participant
alone made him an appropriate choice to facilitate the crossing of Río
Yaqui ceremonial participants into the United States, it is very possible
that ceremonial elders chose him for this task due to his status as an

"educated" Yaqui. Given the perception of Matus as a good student in the U.S. educational system and as someone familiar with the language of U.S. institutions, elder ceremonial leaders may have seen Matus as a good candidate to deal with the increasing bureaucracy of the border. Matus's demonstrated devotion to his ceremonial duties and his proven ability to carry out a task necessary to the continuance of Barrio Libre ceremonies surely made ceremonial elders confident in his ability to serve as a leader in the ceremonial life of the community.

To ensure passage for Río Yaqui ceremonial participants, Matus would establish communication with the U.S. Department of State and the embassy in Hermosillo, Sonora, informing officials on both sides of the U.S.–Mexico border about the movement of Yoeme ceremonial participants across the border. He also solicited the help of elected officials who could support the position that Yaqui ceremonies were a real and important part of cultural life in Arizona. When Matus began facilitating border crossing for Río Yaqui ceremonial participants, Yaqui in Arizona had not yet gained federal recognition as a tribe. However, the Pascua Yaqui Association (PYA), the Arizona Yoeme organization that would eventually push for federal recognition, had already secured federal trust land for Arizona Yoeme as a culturally distinct population.[17] Anselmo Valencia, who played a leading role in PYA organizing and emerged as a Pascua Yaqui community representative, supported Barrio Libre's efforts to bring in Río Yaqui ceremonial participants. Valencia provided Matus with a "letter of recognition" from the PYA identifying Matus as a Yaqui of Barrio Libre and as responsible for escorting Río Yaqui people for Yaqui ceremonies in Tucson.

There has never been a formal policy or official set of border-crossing procedures established in the United States that recognize the sovereign rights of indigenous peoples to maintain traditional activities and contacts across the U.S.–Mexico border. Unlike indigenous people who hold certain protections under the Jay Treaty to move across traditional territories bisected by the U.S.–Canada border, binational peoples' right to cross the U.S.–Mexico border is not recognized through treaty or other legal forms.[18] Matus and other U.S. tribal members who attempt to bring community members from Mexico into the United States for cultural activities must work through the Department of States' procedures for international "cultural exchanges" between U.S. communities and those in foreign nations. The cultural exchange permit application was the process described to Matus when he first accompanied ceremonial participants across the border. The "letter of recognition" that Matus acquired from the PYA clarified for border officials Matus's status as a recognized liaison between cultural organizations participating in an "exchange." Matus's status as a recognized indigenous community leader was of secondary if any concern to border officials.

The lack of formal procedures for indigenous U.S.–Mexico border crossing has resulted in a number of problems for the Yoeme and other indigenous peoples when crossing the border, including the mishandling of sacred items and racial harassment during the final permit interview. As well, Mexican indigenous community members have been detained or denied entry, significantly disrupting ceremonial activities. The absence of formal border and customs guidelines that address the special border-crossing needs of indigenous peoples denies and creates structural obstacles against U.S.–Mexico binational peoplehoods. Positioning Sonora Yoeme as "foreign" in relationship to Arizona Yoeme, and Yoeme ceremonial activities as "exchanges" of foreign cultural practice, denies the continuance of ancestral Yoeme beliefs and practice that transcends a colonially created political border. The notion that Yoeme from Mexico must be "paroled" into the United States when attending ceremonies further positions Sonora Yoeme as criminal and alien among their own people. While the colonial bureaucratic structure of the permit application process forced on the Yoeme repudiates their inherent sovereignty as a people, the ideological enforcement of the Sonora Yoeme as alien "Other" further exacerbates existing notions of nationality-based difference that have developed among many Arizona Yoeme over the course of recent history.

FROM MEXICAN IMMIGRANTS TO AMERICAN INDIANS

When the Yoeme synthesized their political and ceremonial structures with those of the Spanish Jesuits in 1617, the Yoeme's prophesied *wohnaiki pweblplum* (eight sacred towns) emerged: Potam, Vicam, Torim, Bacum, Cocorit, Huirivis, Belem, and Rahum. Despite several, and sometimes violent, periods of conflict with both Spanish authorities and the Mexican Republic, the Yoeme maintained life in the *wohnaiki pweblplum* until the genocidal movement under Porfirio Diaz forced Yoeme out of their traditional communities.

Yoeme who had secured their safety across the U.S.–Mexico border in Arizona began persistent efforts to communicate with Yoeme who remained in Sonora. Despite the creation of the Border Patrol in 1924, and the increasingly restrictive U.S. immigration legislation after 1900, "Mexican immigrants initially were not subject to most of these restrictions."[19] The relative openness of the U.S.–Mexico border during this period greatly contributed to Yoeme efforts to maintain their homelands in Mexico, as well as to the continued transfer of cultural knowledge among the Yoeme in Arizona. Yoeme in Arizona continued to recross the border into Mexico to provide guns, ammunition, and other supplies to Yoeme militants in Mexico, and community members remained informed of Yoeme movement in the homelands.[20]

In the 1930s, Mexican President Lazaro Cárdenas implemented agrarian reforms involving the formation of *ejidos*, or communal lands held in trust by the government. In 1937, Cárdenas responded to Yoeme claims on communally held lands in the Yaqui Valley by establishing the Yaqui *Zona Indígena*. This allowed for the return of many Yoeme to a portion of their homelands and for the reconstruction of the traditional Yoeme social structure and agricultural economy. Traditional Yoeme leaders immediately began the process of resettling and reestablishing the authority of the *wohnaiki pweblplum*. As Sonora Yoeme reconstructed their communities in the hiakim, Yoeme who had migrated to southern Arizona adapted to life in the United States. Initially fearing deportation in compliance with Mexican government requests, Yoeme in Arizona practiced traditional ceremonies in secret and spoke their language only in their small, covertly formed communities. Gradually, the Yoeme in Arizona began to reconstruct a public ceremonial life and would eventually establish their status as an American Indian tribe in the United States as a strategy for economic and cultural survival.

The Pascua Yaqui Reservation, known among Arizona Yoeme as "New Pascua," is located in southern Arizona adjacent to the city of Tucson. In addition to New Pascua, several Yoeme communities formed in southern Arizona following the Yoeme's forced migration north from 1880 to 1910, including what is now known as Old Pascua in central Tucson, Barrio Libre in South Tucson, Yoem Pueblo in Marana, and Guadalupe in the Phoenix area. In the 1960s, Pascua Yaqui Association leaders sought to improve economic conditions for their community members. In 1964, the PYA was successful in obtaining about 202 acres of deeded trust land from the federal government. The newly formed community of New Pascua and its leaders began pursuing federal recognition as a U.S. tribe in 1975. While the individual Arizona Yaqui communities saw themselves as autonomous, some forming their own associations and councils, the PYA actively involved all of the Arizona Yaqui communities in the tribal recognition process. In 1978, the Pascua Yaqui of Arizona gained federal recognition as an American Indian tribe by act of Congress, and the New Pascua Yaqui reservation was established. Obtaining full federal recognition as a tribal nation in the United States required the Yaqui to demonstrate their enduring traditional practices and long history of migration over the Sonora–Arizona border.

When Yaqui in Arizona were recognized as a tribe in 1978, they were granted all federal services and benefits available to members of official tribes; tribal powers of self-government, including jurisdiction over criminal and civil matters within their lands; and reservation status for their trust lands. However, after reviewing the Pascua Yaqui's proposed constitution in 1987, the Bureau of Indian Affairs (BIA) classified the Pascua Yaqui as a "created" tribe, or "a community of adult Indians" who demonstrated knowledge and practice of Native traditions within the United States, but who lacked inherent sovereignty as a historic people indigenous to the country. Over the course of several years, the Pascua Yaqui Tribe, with assistance from the University of Arizona College of Law, sought to demonstrate the Yaqui's right to historic status. In the 1993 congressional hearing held to clarify the status of the Pascua Yaqui Tribe,[21] Yaqui representatives emphasized the Yoeme history of movement across the Greater Southwest. Such statements were necessary to counter the BIA officials' repeated argument to the subcommittee that the Yaqui did not deserve historic status because they first entered the United States as "political refugees."

Issues of both sovereignty and plenary power were central to the congressional hearings held to clarify Pascua Yaqui tribal status. As Chairman of the Subcommittee on Native Affairs Bill Richardson stated, "At the heart of this inquiry is the concept of tribal sovereignty. This concept is the heart and soul of the Federal tribal relationship. Sovereignty is something this committee takes extremely seriously. Tribal sovereignty is inherent, and it is the task of the Congress to acknowledge the existing sovereignty Tribes retain, not to delegate these powers." As a "created" tribe, the Pascua Yaqui's "self-governing powers" were limited to those delegated by the secretary of the Interior. Without powers of "inherent sovereignty," the BIA argued that the Pascua Yaqui did not have the power to carry out a number of activities necessary to self-governance, including levying taxes and regulating law and order on their reservation. Throughout the congressional hearings on the Pascua Yaqui Clarification Act, the subcommittee consistently challenged the BIA's "authority to make a determination as to how much sovereignty a Tribe has."[22] It is clear that Congress's assertion of its plenary power to expand or limit tribal government powers made the Department of Interior's criteria for the designation of "historic" status irrelevant. As Congressman Craig Thomas stated in the *Congressional Record*, "Given the plenary authority of Congress over all facets of Indian Affairs, it seems to me on those rare occasions when we legislatively recognize a tribe—as we did with the Yaqui—we mean that acknowledgement to be full recognition unless we expressly provide otherwise."[23]

There is in fact no language in the criteria used by the BIA for determining "historic" status that specifies that a Native people must hold precolonial ties to lands in the United States. In a 1991 statement by acting director of Tribal Services sent to the Pascua Yaqui tribal chair opposing proposed changes to the tribal constitution, a historic tribe is simply defined as one "that has existed since time immemorial." This definition of historic tribe is contrasted to that of the "created adult Indian community," which designates an American Indian community that has formed after having "resided together on trust land."[24] In other words, a "created tribe" is a type of corporate community that formed when the federal government assigned shared trust land to American Indians who had different traditional forms of culture or sociopolitical organization but who then organized for self-government. Therefore, the BIA categories used to designate tribal status—"created" versus "historic"—were never sufficient to describe the unique situation of the Yaqui as an indigenous population in the United States. The Yaqui of Arizona were most certainly a Native community with shared traditions in existence since time immemorial and a history of self-government prior to their organization on trust land. They most certainly held established ties to a shared homeland where these traditions and history of self-government originated. It was simply the case that they chose to reorganize themselves on U.S.-provided trust land when a return to the Yaqui homelands in Mexico seemed the less viable solution to their existing hardships.[25]

In both BIA and congressional discourse about Native sovereignty during the 1993 congressional hearing to clarify the status of the Pascua Yaqui, we see a colonial logic at work in which the sovereignty of an indigenous people is defined strictly in terms of the U.S. government's power and control over indigenous peoples. Based on its arguments against the inherent sovereignty of the Pascua Yaqui, the BIA's definition of an indigenous people with inherent sovereignty appears to rest on the assumption that such a people would have had to have been present in the continental United States during the period of U.S. colonial settlement. While on legal grounds, it might make sense for the BIA to argue that the government's trust obligations be limited to indigenous peoples who were organized as sociopolitical entities within the United States during that period, the BIA's attempt to deny the Yaqui as a people that "has existed since time immemorial" asserts that no such people could exist beyond the borders of the United States. Congressional representative statements regarding plenary authority over "the existing sovereignty Tribes retain" are no less problematic. While tribal sovereignty may be "at the heart and soul of the Federal tribal relationship," at the heart of the federal–tribal relationship is the guardian–ward relationship.

As an introduction to the clarification hearing, Congressman Richardson highlighted the third maxim of federal Indian law: "Tribes retain all sovereignty not expressly divested by Congress." Richardson's prefatory statement emphasizes both plenary power and the bind that indigenous peoples find themselves in when asserting their sovereignty rights through federal Indian law. "As evident in the earliest articulations of U.S. law of American Indian tribal sovereignties as 'domestic dependent nations,' tribes in the United States have been paradoxically understood as still bearing an authority that existed prior to the U.S. Constitution, yet is subject today to the actions of a federal government that claims 'sovereignty and dominion' over them as colonized peoples."[26] As Williams argues, legal precedents from the colonial era regarding American Indian rights in the United States continue to limit interpretations of Indian rights and perpetuate the colonial notion of white supremacy over indigenous peoples.[27] Federal Indian law recognizes indigenous peoples as "nations" within a nation with an "inherent sovereignty" that has existed since "time immemorial," creating the illusion of fully preserved precolonial indigenous political power. One must not forget, however, the origins and development of such language within British law and colonial engagement.[28] As dependent "tribes," rather than independent peoples, federally recognized tribes hold a peculiar form of sovereignty, a form of self-governance that is persistently held in check by and subordinate to the desires of the federal government.

Tribal recognition in 1978 and clarification of historic tribe status in 1994 contributed greatly to the Arizona Yoeme's ability to survive both economically and culturally within the United States. Enrolled Pascua Yaqui members residing on the reservation, as well as those residing in Arizona Yaqui communities such as Barrio Libre, have benefited from federally supported tribal services. Funds for Yaqui cultural revitalization projects and the extension of tribal services to non-reservation Yaqui communities have certainly assisted in both the maintenance of Yoeme cultural knowledge in the United States and a sense of Yaqui community beyond reservation lands. Yet, tribal recognition has also resulted in significant changes to Arizona Yoeme sociopolitical organization and the ability of traditional leadership to participate in policy decisions affecting Yoeme cultural preservation. This situation is illustrated by the marginalization of traditional leadership in tribal border-crossing policy, which is shaped both by federal imposition and emerging notions of a U.S. tribal identity that is distinct from that of the Sonora Yoeme.

DIVIDED YOEME

Following tribal recognition of the Pascua Yaqui in 1978, Matus would continue to work with other ceremonial leaders, both in Barrio Libre and the other Arizona Yaqui communities, to bring Río Yaqui ceremonial participants into the United States. Matus observes that there were no immediate or major changes to life in the Yaqui community following recognition, and there were no immediate changes to the process involved in facilitating transborder ceremonial organizing. A shift in this process would come with both increased U.S. border enforcement beginning in the 1990s and changing perceptions of Yaqui authority. The passage of the Immigration Act of 1990 and the Illegal Immigration Reform and Immigration Responsibility Act in 1996 resulted in a massive increase in U.S. border enforcement. In the early nineties, Border Patrol strategies such as Operation Gatekeeper in San Diego, California, Operation Hold the Line in El Paso, Texas, and Operation Safeguard in Nogales, Arizona, focused on deterring illegal entrance at U.S.–Mexico urban ports of entry. Such strategies funneled the movement of illegal traffic through rural entry points, and the late nineties saw an increased focus on Border Patrol manpower, surveillance, and barrier construction along the entire stretch of the U.S.–Mexico border. At this time, Matus was still able to bring in Río Yaqui ceremonial participants, working through the same channels and procedures he had been following since the early seventies. The ceremonial groups, however, faced increased questioning by border officials, and significant delays and denials of entry when crossing the Nogales port of entry for ceremonies.

In 1997, Matus began to involve the Pascua Yaqui Tribal Council in the process of facilitating border crossing for Sonora Yaqui ceremonial participants. As Matus states:

> I figured that it was going to be easier for me to involve
> the council in this process because of that mandate that
> the tribal government had with the federal government.
> I think it was a mistake for me to do that, because I did
> have the authority to bring in people. Well, you see, traditionally, you should have that authority. But my concern
> was that then the federal government was getting tougher
> and tougher on immigration, that at some point they were
> going to try to put a stop to it, because we're not part of
> the government. The Yaqui community where I'm from
> is not on the reservation. So, they would say, "Well, we
> cannot help you anymore with bringing in people without
> documents. We're going to have to have a letter from your
> tribal council or have your tribal council do this."

While Matus believes that it was "premature" for him to have sought the support of tribal council since Border Patrol had not yet expressed the need for tribal government approvals, tribal council involvement seems to have been inevitable.

In 1997, Matus began working with the Yoemem Tekia Foundation, a nonprofit Yaqui cultural heritage organization located on the Pascua Yaqui Reservation. At the time, Matus was helping New Pascua ceremonial leaders bring in community members from Río Yaqui. While negotiating on conditions of crossing with the embassy in Hermosillo, Matus suggested that Yoemem Tekia be acknowledged as the lead organization for the Yaqui community in bringing Yaqui from Mexico into the United States, "with the approval of the ceremonial leaders." Since Yoemem Tekia is a grassroots cultural organization located on tribal lands, it seemed the logical choice as lead organization for Yaqui border crossing, if issues of tribal representation were to arise. Yoemem Tekia took the lead in facilitating border crossing for the next few years, but by 2000, the Pascua Yaqui Tribal Council had expressed concern about the grassroots group handling Yaqui affairs at the border. Matus states:

> That's when the tribal council says, "Well, we'll do all the paperwork. We'll do all this, and we'll do all the negotiating for you guys. And we'll involve you guys." And they did in the beginning . . . now they just do things on their own . . . they don't invite the ceremonial leaders anymore. They just do their own thing, and then they tell us, "Well, this is what the government wants." You know? So that's how it got out of our hands . . . now the tribal council says, "We have the authority and you don't."

Following the 9/11 attacks and the creation of the Department of Homeland Security (DHS), the federal government would insist that tribal governments alone had the authority to negotiate the crossing of non–U.S. citizen indigenous relatives into the United States. In 2003, Immigration and Naturalization Services (INS) was replaced by the Department of Homeland Security's Immigration and Customs Enforcement (ICE) and Citizenship and Immigration Services (CIS). As a result, Border Patrol, along with the INS and U.S. Customs inspection divisions, was absorbed by a new DHS agency called Customs and Border Protection (CBP). When this change occurred, Matus faced difficulties in obtaining a meeting with new DHS agency officials in order to discuss any new procedures that ceremonial leaders would need to be aware of when crossing the border with Río Yaqui ceremonial participants. Eventually, DHS officials would arrange for a meeting with Yaqui tribal officials to discuss Yaqui border-crossing issues, but ceremonial leaders were excluded from this meeting. For Matus, this moment marked a clear shift from the recognition of ceremonial leaders' authority as a part of tribal governance to the complete bureaucratic authority of tribal council. In the Yoeme oral tradition, the phrase "like this it stays in your hands" expresses a Yoeme listener's inheritance of Yoeme traditional knowledge and truth, as well as the responsibility to care for this inheritance. Whether intentional or not, Matus's statement about Yoeme border crossing getting "out of our hands" aptly expresses Matus's sense of loss in the ceremonial leaders' ability to maintain their Yoeme inheritance as they are marginalized in government-to-government negotiations over a critical issue related to ceremonial preservation.

In a 2008 interview, Matus describes an incident at the border that demonstrates the heightened suspicions and power to deny entry among CBP officials, as well as the shift to Yaqui bureaucratic authority. When crossing the border with a Yaqui ceremonial group, one of the ceremonial participants was red-flagged when his name was entered in the CBP system during the permit application process. When crossing the border on a previous visit, this individual was found with a pay stub indicating that he had worked in Arizona during one of his visits. When the pay stub was discovered, this individual was prohibited from reentering the United States for the period of one year. In accordance with this suspension, this individual did not participate in Arizona Yaqui ceremonies nor attempt to reenter the United States on his own for over a year. Despite expiration of the suspension, however, border officials were reluctant to allow this individual to reenter the United States for ceremonies during the final interview at the border.

Knowing that this individual was needed for the upcoming Barrio Libre ceremonies, Matus attempted to negotiate the terms of this ceremonial participant's stay in the United States. However, CBP officials insisted that Matus would "have to get the okay" from his "ceremonial elder." Matus, who is the eldest ceremonial leader of Barrio Libre responsible for bringing in ceremonial participants, responded, "What ceremonial elder?" The CBP agent clarified that he was referring to the Pascua Yaqui Tribal Council representative who was listed as the Yaqui tribal authority in their system.

After speaking with this tribal authority, the border official reported to Matus, "He says you have no authority," and that the individual in question would not be allowed entry into the United States. Matus contacted the tribal authority directly, and attempted to explain why the red-flagged ceremonial participant was not being allowed entry and why it was necessary to negotiate his stay in Barrio Libre. In response, the tribal official clearly indicated his belief that the red-flagged ceremonial participant should not be granted entry because of his past offense. It was troubling to Matus that this tribal official passed judgment on a ceremonial participant's status based solely on information received from border officials. Matus was also deeply disturbed by the council member's choice of words to describe the Sonora Yaqui ceremonial participant—"dirty." Although the term may have been used to describe the individual's indiscretions regarding previous wage-earning work in the United States, Matus was reminded of the term's use by Anglos in the earlier years of his youth to describe Yaqui both as "dirty Indians" and "dirty Mexicans." Now the term was being used by an American Yaqui community leader to describe a Yaqui community member.

Matus believes that such statements, revealing an Anglo or Western view of "Mexicans" among Arizona Yaqui, further indicates a divide in the Arizona Yaqui community between traditional and nontraditional (Western) ways of understanding Yoeme practices and people:

> Well, you have the traditional Yaquis and the non-traditional Yaquis. And that's where the dividing line comes, where you have the traditional people who know and recognize their relatives in Mexico, and their concern is keeping contact with them, or being able to cross the border, and have them come to visit.
>
> With the non-traditional Yaquis, it's, "I'm an American. They're Mexicans. And they may be related, but I'm from here and they're from there, so there's no problem" . . . It doesn't matter to them. They don't see that as a big deal. "If the United States wants to fence up the entire southern border, let them do it. It's not important to me." You know? That's the type of mentality we have to deal with oftentimes.

Pascua Yaqui activists from the Yoeme Commission on Human Rights express a similar concern. When discussing why so few Pascua Yaqui community members participate in grassroots-organized goodwill trips to Río Yaqui, commission members expressed their belief that most Pascua Yaqui simply "don't care" about Yoeme in Mexico. The sense of detachment from Yaqui in Mexico felt by many Pascua Yaqui is also reflected in limited tribal support for Pascua Yaqui ceremonial leaders in bringing across "Mexicans" for ceremonial events. The Pascua Yaqui tribe does, in fact, provide support for several transborder cultural projects, such as the inclusion of Río Yaqui traditional healers in the tribe's Alternative Medicine Clinic and its community health fairs. The tribe has also recently provided funds and transportation for Yaqui elders in Arizona to attend religious festivals in Mexico. Some support in the form of tribal vehicle use has also been granted to grassroots-initiated projects such as the Yoeme commission's annual goodwill trips, although grassroots groups are largely responsible for fundraising in and out of the Yaqui community to cover the majority of costs for such projects. Ceremonial leaders like Matus are provided tribal vehicles on request and some funds to help cover transportation and application fees for the entrance of Río Yaqui ceremonial participants, although the funds provided typically do not cover the full costs of travel and fees.

The primary concern for ceremonial leaders like Matus, however, is that the tribal government has not provided them with true political support in their efforts to include Río Yaqui participants in community ceremonies. As the incident at the border described above demonstrates, Yaqui ceremonial leaders cannot necessarily count on the support of tribal government officials when making decisions at the border. The tribal council has also been reluctant to form resolutions that would establish an official tribal office or program for dealing with border-crossing issues, or official designations that would grant recognized ceremonial leaders the authority to negotiate the entrance of Río Yaqui ceremonial participants at the border. Ceremonial leaders charged with transborder ceremonial organizing are, therefore, forced to carry out their responsibilities within the colonially derived frameworks of both federal border policy and tribal governance, both of which erase their traditional authority to collaborate with other Yoeme authorities in policy-related decisions relevant to Yoeme border crossing.

The lack of tribal government support in addressing border-crossing problems for ceremonial participants may result from a combination of a Westernized view of "Mexican" Yoeme and concern over tribal funding. The tribal council has been reluctant to accept proposals that push for the recognition of Yaqui binational citizenship or binational tribal membership in order to facilitate Yaqui cross-border ties. Objections to Yaqui binational citizenship within the Arizona Yaqui community mirror objections posed by other U.S. Native groups to Yaqui tribal recognition in the seventies. Several U.S. Native communities opposed the Yaqui petition for federal recognition, arguing that recognition of "Mexican Indians" would unfairly distribute funds reserved for tribes indigenous to the continental United States.[29] A similar argument is now present among Arizona Yaqui who fear that already limited tribal funding might be more thinly spread among a large Yaqui population in Mexico. For some traditional leaders like Matus, the greater fear is that tribally governed economic development will increasingly disrupt the traditional ceremonial life of the community:

> When the Yaquis became recognized as an American
> Indian tribe that thinking started about how are we going
> to make money and how are we going to survive. Instead
> of promoting the ceremonies and Yaqui ways, we were
> promoting being organized and educated in . . . economic
> development. I'm not totally against economic develop-
> ment but I think that has disrupted a lot in the Yaqui com-
> munity. It has disrupted the thinking of a lot of our elders,
> a lot of our youth . . . There has to be a way that we can
> balance the economics over here and the culture over
> here. But right now, it's . . . economics over here and cul-
> ture at the bottom. It's not balanced.

Matus believes that the inability to balance ceremonial life with economic development will lead to a substantial loss of Yaqui traditional knowledge and cultural life, unless traditional people are able to strengthen their connections and reach across the U.S.–Mexico divide.

CONCLUSION

Fears over cultural loss related to the strict enforcement of the U.S.–Mexico border are not only a concern for the Yoeme, but for numerous indigenous peoples in the U.S.–Mexico border region.[30] In August 1997, members of various U.S.–Mexico border indigenous communities gathered at the Tohono O'odham Nation's cultural center to discuss their concerns over how border policy could impact their traditional lifeways. The Alianza Indígena Sin Fronteras was formed as a result of this gathering. José Matus continues to serve as the organization's project director. The grassroots group's banner reads, "Somos una famila; no tenemos fronteras" / "We are one family; we have no borders."

Article 36 of the United Nations Declaration on the Rights of Indigenous Peoples (UNDRIP) states, "Indigenous Peoples, in particular those divided by international borders, have the right to maintain and develop contact, relations and cooperation, including activities for spiritual, cultural, political, economic and social purposes, with other peoples across borders."[31] Six months before the UNDRIP's adoption by the UN General Assembly in 2007, a number of indigenous activists and leaders met in Phoenix, Arizona, for a community forum with Wilton Littlechild, at that time the North American representative of the UN Permanent Forum on Indigenous Issues. While hopeful of the UNDRIP's possible impact on border policy and indigenous border rights, Matus shared pessimism at the forum about the declaration's influence on tribal government decision making. Matus recalled arguing to a Yaqui tribal council member that the tribe should negotiate with the federal government to better secure border-crossing rights for Yoeme in Mexico, given the establishment of such rights in international law. According to Matus, the tribal council member responded that international law "doesn't mean anything for tribes" and therefore "doesn't matter." In a sense, the Yaqui council member was correct. International law has no binding force in a nation unless recognized by its constitution, resolutions, or domestic court decisions. This is why indigenous international rights activists have encouraged both tribal governments and state legislatures to adopt the UNDRIP. The Arizona State Legislature adopted the UNDRIP in March 2007, and the Salt River Pima-Maricopa Indian Community and the Gila River Indian Community in Arizona were among the first tribal nations to adopt the declaration by tribal resolution.[32]

It has not been the intent of this essay to criticize the Pascua Yaqui Tribe for its policies regarding the border-crossing rights of Yoeme in Mexico. A Pascua Yaqui tribal resolution committed to preserving border-crossing rights as described in the UNDRIP and to empowering Arizona Yaqui ceremonial leaders to negotiate on the behalf of Yoeme ceremonial participants from Mexico might facilitate Yoeme cross-border connections. More importantly, it would recognize and promote the traditional authority of Yoeme ceremonial leadership as well as the importance of Yoeme transborder connections. It is not clear, however, that such tribal resolutions would provide the Pascua Yaqui Tribe with the negotiating power sufficient to truly transform border-crossing policies for Yoeme in Mexico and secure the future of cross-border cultural preservation efforts. In light of the Secure Fence Act of 2006, the U.S. administration's dedication to increasing border security as a central aspect of immigration reform, and apparent problems in training agents and maintaining transparency in an ever-growing Customs and Border Protection force,[33] U.S. tribal nations at the U.S.–Mexico border appear to have very limited power when it comes to decisions regarding border-crossing procedures.

The primary goal of this essay has been to address the impacts of current U.S.–Mexico border policies, both federal and tribal, on contemporary Yoeme peoplehood. Like all peoples in the U.S.–Mexico border region, Yoeme identities and political perspectives are shaped by dominant ideologies regarding national and ethnic "Others." Although there is much that still unites Yoeme across the U.S.–Mexico border, the fragmentation of experience among Yoeme individuals has resulted in ideological border reinforcement,[34] whereby Yoeme on one side of the border imagine those on the other side in terms of "the Other." Pascua Yaqui tribal leadership decisions that seem to conflict with some traditionalist perspectives on Yoeme transborder movements should, therefore, be seen as a representation of broader Yaqui perspectives and interests in Arizona. Yet, from a peoplehood perspective, it seems that the weakening of Yoeme transborder connections threatens Yoeme peoplehood by further fragmenting Yoeme knowledge and practice across the Yoeme binational landscape. Transnational Yoeme ties are weakened by a combination of federal border enforcement measures, the limited power of tribal governments to negotiate the terms of indigenous border movement, the marginalization of ceremonial leadership in tribal governance, and dominant ideologies enforcing notions of national difference. For this reason, the grassroots border rights activism of ceremonial leaders such as Matus may someday be viewed in historical perspective as an important movement for continued Yoeme persistence.

AUTHOR BIOGRAPHY

Christina Leza (Yoeme/Chicana) is an assistant professor of anthropology at Colorado College and core faculty in the Southwest Studies and Race, Ethnicity, and Migration Studies programs.

1 Yoeme, meaning "the people," is the traditional term used by the Yoeme to identify themselves. The community was first called the Yaqui by the Spanish, and since this has become the common term used by non-Yoeme to describe them, Yoeme on both sides of the border often identify themselves as Yaqui, particularly when communicating with outsiders to the community. I privilege the traditional term Yoeme in this essay but occasionally use Yaqui because of its continued common usage in and out of the Yoeme community and to clearly identify the federally recognized Pascua Yaqui Nation.

2 "Porfiriato" refers to the Mexican historical period, 1876 to 1911, in which Porfirio Diaz maintained power as president of Mexico. Centralizing the government, Diaz instituted a land reform program that focused on privatization and included policies on indigenous "extermination" in cases of indigenous resistance. See Guillermo Bonfil Batalla, *Mexico Profundo: Reclaiming a Civilization* (Austin: University of Texas Press, 1996); Shelley B. Hatfield, *Chasing Shadows: Indians along the United States–Mexico Border, 1876–1911* (Albuquerque: University of New Mexico Press, 1998); and T. G. Powell, "Mexican Intellectuals and the Indian Question, 1876–1911," *Hispanic Historical Review* 48, no. 1 (1968): 19–36.

3 Edward H. Spicer, *Pascua: A Yaqui Village in Arizona* (Chicago: University of Chicago Press, 1940), 4.

4 Tom Holm, J. Diane Pearson, and Ben Chavis, "Peoplehood: A Model for the Extension of Sovereignty in American Indian Studies," *Wicazo Sa Review* 18, no. 1 (2003): 7–24.

5 Edward H. Spicer, *Potam: A Yaqui Village in Sonora* (American Anthropological Association, 1954),

55; Kirsten C. Erickson, "Lonely Ranchers, Solitary Students, and Angry Governors: Vulnerability and Community Conflict in Yaqui Emotion Talk," *Western Folklore* 68, no. 1 (2009): 27–48.

6 Spicer, *Potam*, 96.

7 Erickson, "Lonely Ranchers, Solitary Students, and Angry Governors," 34.

8 Ibid., 33–38. For a discussion of "progressive/traditional" conflict among the Sonora Yoeme, also see David D. Shorter, *We Will Dance Our Truth: Yaqui History in Yoeme Performances* (Lincoln: University of Nebraska Press, 2009), 70–72; and Pamela Hartman, "Yaqui Tribe's Factional Dispute Turns Bloody," *Tucson Citizen*, November 25, 1994, http://tucsoncitizen.com/morgue2/1994/11/25/208840-yaqui-tribe-s-factional-dispute-turns-bloody/.

9 Robert R. Alvarez Jr., "The Mexican–U.S. Border: The Making of an Anthropology of Borderlands," *Annual Review of Anthropology* 24 (1995): 453; Edward H. Spicer, *Cycles of Conquest: The Impact of Spain, Mexico, and the United States on Indians of the Southwest* (Tucson: University of Arizona Press, 1962).

10 Edward H. Spicer, "Persistent Cultural Systems: A Comparative Study of Identity Systems That Can Adapt to Contrasting Environments," *Science* 174 (1971): 795–800; George Pierre Castile and Gilbert Kushner, *Persistent Peoples: Cultural Enclaves in Perspective* (Washington, D.C.: George Washington University Institute for Ethnographic Research, 1981).

11 Kirsten C. Erickson, *Yaqui Homeland and Homeplace: The Everyday Production of Ethnic Identity* (Tucson: University of Arizona Press, 2008); Shorter, *We Will Dance Our Truth*.

12 Evelyn Hu-DeHart, *Yaqui Resistance and Survival: The Struggle for Land and Autonomy, 1821–1910* (Madison: University of Wisconsin Press, 1984); Edward Spicer, *The Yaquis: A Cultural History* (Tucson: University of Arizona Press, 1980).

13 Muriel T. Painter, *With Good Heart: Yaqui Beliefs and Ceremonies in Pascua Village* (Tucson: University of Arizona Press, 1986).

14 Pascola, or pahko'ola, means "old man of the ceremony." The pascola dancer is of pre-Columbian origin. His ceremonial dance is accompanied by musicians including the *tampaleo* (ceremonial flute and drum player), violinist, and harp player.

15 Matus estimates that recruitment of Río Yaqui ceremonial participants began in the 1930s. This time period coincides with the return of Sonora Yaqui to their homelands, which would have made contact between ceremonial participants easier and increased the ability of Yaqui ceremonial participants to cross into the United States safely.

16 The deer dancer, *saila maso* (little brother deer), is central to Yoeme ceremonial life. Deer songs and deer dances are associated with the *sea anía* or *seyewailo* (flower world), the aspect of Yoeme cosmology associated with the Yoemes' most ancient ancestors. See Larry Evers and Felipe S. Molina, *Yaqui Deer Songs/Maso Bwikam: A Native American Poetry* (Tucson: University of Arizona Press, 1987).

17 George Pierre Castile, "Yaquis, Edward H. Spicer, and Federal Indian Policy: From Immigrants to Native Americans," *Journal of the Southwest* 44, no. 4 (2002): 383–435; Mark E. Miller, "The Yaquis Become Americans: The Process of Federal Tribal Recognition," *Journal of Arizona History* 65 (1994): 183–204; and Mark E. Miller, *Forgotten Tribes: Unrecognized Indians and the Federal Acknowledgement Process* (Lincoln: University of Nebraska Press, 2004), 79–122.

18 The Kickapoo are an exception. The Texas Band of Kickapoo Act passed by Congress in 1983 specifies that "all members of the Band," regardless of citizenship, "shall be entitled to freely pass and repass the borders of the United States and to live and work in the United States" (25 U.S.C. § 1300b-13).

19 David G. Gutierrez, *Walls and Mirrors: Mexican Americans, Mexican Immigrants, and the Politics of Ethnicity* (Berkeley: University of California Press, 1995), 52.

20 Larry Evers and Felipe S. Molina, *Hiakim: The Yaqui Homeland*, special edition of *Journal of the Southwest* 34, no. 1 (1992).

21 U.S. Congress, House of Representatives, Subcommittee on Native American Affairs of the Committee on Natural Resources, *Pascua Yaqui Status Clarification Act Hearing*, 103rd Congress, 1st session, April 30, 1993, http://archive.org/stream/pascuayaquistatu00unit/pascuayaquistatu00unit_djvu.txt.

22 Congressman Richardson, *Pascua Yaqui Clarification Act Hearing*.

23 Congressman Thomas, speaking on amendments to H.R. 734, 103rd Congress, *Congressional Record* (August 2, 1993): H 5633.

24 David Eugene Wilkins and Heidi Kiiwetinepinesiik Stark, *American Indian Politics and the American Political System* (Lanham, Md.: Rowman & Littlefield, 2011), 6. When Congress acknowledged the Pascua Yaqui as a tribe in 1978, the BIA acknowledgment procedures neither distinguished between

a historic tribe and "created tribe" nor described what criteria would be used to create such a distinction.

25 For a more detailed discussion on the poor economic conditions faced by Yaqui in Arizona and the need for federal funds to support continued cultural survival of the Yaqui in the United States, see Miller, *Forgotten Tribes*, 83–90.

26 Justin B. Richland, *Arguing with Tradition: The Language of Law in Hopi Tribal Court* (Chicago: University of Chicago Press, 2008), 4.

27 Robert A. Williams Jr., *Like a Loaded Weapon: The Rehnquist Court, Indian Rights, and the Legal History of Racism in America* (Minneapolis: University of Minnesota Press, 2005).

28 Richard Perry, *Time Immemorial: Indigenous Peoples and State Systems* (Austin: University of Texas Press, 1996).

29 Castile, "Yaquis, Edward H. Spicer, and Federal Indian Policy," 405–6; Miller, "The Yaquis Become Americans."

30 For an overview of border-crossing issues faced by indige-nous peoples at the northern and southern U.S. borders, see Eileen Luna-Firebaugh, "The Border Crossed Us: Border Crossing Issues of the Indigenous Peoples of the Americas," *Wicazo Sa Review* 17, no. 1 (2002): 159–81.

31 http://www.un.org/esa/socdev/unpfii/documents/DRIPS_en.pdf.

32 Shannon Rivers, "Gila River Indian Community Becomes First Tribal Nation to Embrace U.N. Declarations on the Rights of Indigenous Peoples," *Barriozona*, http://www.barriozona.com/gila_river_first_to_embrace_united_nations_declaration_shannon_rivers.html.

33 "Impunity and the Border Patrol," *The New York Times*, May 11, 2014; "A New Border Patrol Chief Signals He Is Ready to End a Culture of Impunity," *The Washington Post*, July 25, 2014; and Brian Bennett, "Border Patrol's Use of Deadly Force Criticized in Report," *Los Angeles Times*, February 27, 2014.

34 Pablo Vila, *Crossing Borders/Re-inforcing Borders: Social Categories, Metaphors, and Narrative Identities on the U.S.–Mexico Frontier* (Austin: University of Texas Press, 2000).

"This Is the Nation's Heart-String"
Formal Education and the Cherokee Diaspora during the Late Nineteenth and Early Twentieth Centuries

Gregory D. Smithers

On March 10, 1881, the *Cherokee Orphan Asylum Press* published an editorial by Walter Adair Duncan. Duncan, the superintendent of the Cherokee Orphan Asylum between 1872 and 1884 and one of the leading Cherokee intellectuals of his era, offered heartfelt praise for the Cherokee Nation's system of public education.[1] At the time of Duncan's editorial, the Cherokee Nation in Indian Territory operated over one hundred day schools, a Cherokee male and Cherokee female seminary, and an orphanage.[2] Duncan insisted that due to these institutions "no people in the world are better situated than the Cherokees." He added that the true value of formal education lay in how it gave meaning to "national life." As Duncan stated this point, "This [formal education] is the nation's heart-string. It is the jeweled chord that binds the people together into a national whole, attaching them to one another, to home and to the land in which they were born."[3]

Declarations of this nature highlighted two important realities for Cherokee people at the turn of the nineteenth and twentieth century. First, the Cherokees were a scattered people, exiled from their southeastern homeland by the forces of settler colonialism that culminated with the United States' violent removal of Cherokee people to Indian Territory in 1838 and 1839. In the decades following removal, the Cherokees rebuilt their lives in the trans-Mississippi West, and throughout North America (and sometimes beyond). The exiled and scattered nature of the Cherokees, hallmarks of a diasporic people, saw

Cherokee leaders in Indian Territory value education as a means of connecting widely dispersed Cherokee individuals, families, and communities. Thus the second critical reality of the Cherokee people: its leaders—men like William Adair Duncan—valued formal education as a means of reimagining Cherokee identity: a nationalistic Cherokee identity that connected a diasporic people to a political homeland in Indian Territory.[4]

Historians of the Cherokee people—and Native Americans more generally—rarely view indigenous histories through the lens of diaspora. This is certainly true of the historical scholarship about the Cherokee people and the education system they developed. Scholars such as Devon Mihesuah and Marilyn Holt have focused on how the exiled Cherokees in Indian Territory, like the neighboring Creek, Seminole, Choctaw, and Chickasaw, founded their own educational institutions in the trans-Mississippi West in the decades following the forced removals of the 1830s.[5] For leading proponents of public education in the Cherokee Nation, the National Council's support of a formal system of education played a vital role in raising "intelligent Cherokee children, trained for useful occupations, who love their country."[6]

The expression of such nationalistic sentiments among the diasporic Cherokees in Indian Territory reached their highest pitch during the 1880s as Euro-American "sooners" and "boomers" carved out homesteads on the "Unassigned Lands" of Indian Territory. The growing populations of Euro-Americans in and around Indian Territory reinforced political calls for the termination of Native sovereignty and communal landholdings, and the divvying up of that land in individual allotments. The Dawes and Curtis Acts (1887 and 1898, respectively) ultimately paved the way for these shifts in American Indian policy to become a reality. For the Cherokees, severalty and allotment brought an end to Cherokee-run government, and, significantly, the loss of control over the public system of education deemed the "heart-string" of a dispersed people and a source of nationalistic pride in their trans-Mississippi homeland. Thus, by 1900 the Cherokee people's institutions of education came under the control of "a Superintendent for the territory and a tribe supervisor, appointed by the US Government."[7] Unlike leaders of the Cherokee Nation in Indian Territory who set out to use education to inspire children with a nationalistic love for the Cherokee Nation, federal government officials aimed to erode such feelings and to instead use education to assimilate American Indians to white society by redirecting their nationalistic affections toward the United States.[8]

The Cherokee Nation's loss of control over their own educational institutions in Indian Territory (what became part of the state of Oklahoma after November 16, 1907) represented a massive blow for Cherokee leaders dedicated to nurturing Cherokee national identity on land far from their ancestral homeland in the Southeast. As far as U.S. officials saw matters, however, assimilationist education constituted a humanitarian and progressive policy. Indeed, Christian missionaries (a large proportion of whom were Quakers) and the federal government developed a relatively close working relationship after the American Civil War and brought religious and federally operated schools to the Cherokees living on their ancestral homeland in North Carolina, and in federally run off-reservation boarding schools throughout the United States. These educational facilities aimed to assimilate American Indian children to white society, or as historian David Wallace Adams puts it, "to completely restructure the Indians' minds and personalities."[9]

However, formal education, whether received in the Cherokee ancestral homeland in the Southeast, the Cherokee Nation in Indian Territory prior to 1900, or throughout the United States, did provide Cherokees with practical skills to make a living, and to read, write, and correspond with one another. Formal education also provided Cherokees with new ways to think creatively about what it meant to be a Cherokee living in, for example, Tahlequah, Oklahoma; Cherokee, North Carolina; or Riverside, California. Formal education thus provided Cherokee youths with something tangible (the skills to make a living and support a family), and creative (the ability to communicate, share stories, and continue the process of reimagining what it meant to be a Cherokee living in diaspora). Despite all of the limitations associated with the different forms of education available to Cherokee children at the turn of the nineteenth and twentieth century, formal education provided Cherokees with some basic skills for making a living and exposed young people to new forms of knowledge that might enable them to stitch together a diasporic sense of community and belonging within the settler societies of the United States.

This essay focuses on the educational institutions that Cherokee children experienced in the Cherokee Nation in Indian Territory, at the North Carolina Cherokees' Qualla Reservation, and at the Sherman Institute, an off-reservation boarding school located in Riverside, California, and administered by the federal government's Bureau of Indian Affairs (BIA). Guiding my analysis is a set of questions: To what degree did these varied educational experiences reinforce the metaphor of a "jeweled chord" binding Cherokees together? Alternatively, did the range of institutional experiences located outside of the Cherokee Nation work to sever the "heart-string," or the emotional and nationalistic pride that Cherokees felt for the Cherokee Nation in Indian Territory? As my analysis reveals, not all of the institutions discussed in this essay were "jewels," while the education received in the various institutions did not always unite Cherokee people or brighten the heartstrings with feelings of emotional connectedness to a nationalistic Cherokee identity.

FROM NATION TO DIASPORA:
A FRAMEWORK

To begin to answer the above questions, it is important to first note that historians routinely highlight the importance of the nation-state framework in nineteenth- and early twentieth-century Cherokee history. There are good reasons for this. The Cherokee adopted a nation-state model during the early nineteenth century, a model that historian Mary Young famously claimed "mirrored" that of the American republic.[10] Subsequent scholarship by William McLoughlin and Andrew Denson, to name just two prominent examples, developed our historical understanding of the importance of Cherokee sovereignty and nationalism, and the relationship of these concepts to the evolution of Cherokee civic and political identity during the nineteenth and early twentieth centuries.[11]

The Cherokee's development of centralized government constituted a significant departure from traditional town- and clan-based systems of governance.[12] Prior to the development of centralized institutions during the early nineteenth century, Cherokee education was received in one's town and revolved around elders passing down origin narratives, legends, medicinal knowledge, and beliefs about the spirit world. Oral forms of knowledge—which persisted during the nineteenth century as a small Cherokee elite began centralizing and bureaucratizing almost every facet of life in the Cherokee Nation, first in the Southeast and then in Indian Territory—created a very different sense of history and time for Cherokees. In contrast to the linear traditions common to Western cultures, Cherokees traditionally educated children about the honored place that past events, places, spirits, and knowledge had in Cherokee life, and how this knowledge impacted life in the present. Thus, unlike Western intellectual traditions, which places cultural distance between the past and the present, Cherokee children learned of the connected nature of history, just as they learned about the connectedness of all living souls.[13]

As Cherokee social and political life changed following the arrival of Europeans, so Cherokees reimagined traditional beliefs and educational practices to meet the demands of settler colonialism. By the 1790s, an emerging generation of Cherokee leaders began taking a radical approach to dealing with the pressures of Euro-American colonialism and changes to traditional modes of life. In the wake of the American Revolutionary War, Cherokees began reorienting towns (most of which were razed to the ground during the revolutionary era) and living increasingly on communal farmsteads, while the matrilineal clan system slowly gave way to a Cherokee system of patriarchy, written laws, and centralized government. Amid these changes, some Cherokees—such as Oolootekea (known to Euro-Americans as John

Jolly), Connetoo (or John Hill), and Tachee (or Dutch)—chose not to be part of the nation emerging in the woodland South and began migrating westward to the Arkansas Valley and Mexican Texas. These Cherokees were the vanguard of a diaspora that eventually numbered in the thousands following the federal government's forced relocation of the Cherokee Nation in 1838 and 1839.[14]

What became known as the "Trail of Tears" constituted the most famous migration of Cherokee people. In 1838 and 1839, the federal government forced an estimated 12,000 to 15,000 Cherokees from their homes and farms in the Southeast to land reserved for them in Indian Territory. By 1840, only about 1,100 Cherokees remained on what Cherokees considered their "ancient homeland" in the Great Smoky Mountains.[15] As a result of removal, then, the Cherokee people effectively had two homelands by the 1840s. Cherokees throughout North America looked to the Qualla Boundary reservation in the Great Smoky Mountains with great fondness, viewing it as an important connection to their ancestral homeland. In the trans-Mississippi West, where most Cherokees now lived, the Cherokee Nation in Indian Territory became the political homeland of the Cherokee diaspora.

American colonialism had therefore played a significant role in transforming the Cherokee into a diasporic people.[16] Those Cherokee leaders with responsibility for overseeing the rebuilding of Cherokee communities in the trans-Mississippi West viewed formal education as vital to cultivating Cherokee minds, nourishing Cherokee souls, and unifying an exiled people. As well, uniting a diasporic people in a common Cherokee identity required a language. That language was English.

Cherokee people took great pride in Sequoyah's invention of the Cherokee syllabary in the early nineteenth century. Indeed, the Cherokee language continued to be spoken in the mountains of North Carolina and in Indian Territory throughout the nineteenth and into the early twentieth centuries.[17] According to Cherokee educators, however, a common language of instruction was crucial to nurturing basic skills in numeracy, literacy, geography, and history, and, not insignificantly, to contradicting Euro-American stereotypes about the intellectual capabilities of Native American people. As such, English became the dominant language of instruction in Cherokee schools, and certainly in educational facilities operated by Christian missionaries and the federal government. In the Cherokee Nation in Indian Territory, for example, English was the preferred language of instruction for the mixed-race Cherokee teachers who far outnumbered white teachers in the common schools, seminaries, and orphanages.[18] The preference for English language instruction was certainly a controversial choice. The extermination of Native American languages was seen by white educators of indigenous children as one of the fastest ways in which to assimilate American Indians into white society.[19] The

mixed-race Cherokee educators working in the Cherokee Nation's educational facilities appear to have had hopes of inverting that formula,
using English literacy instead to nurture a sense of nationalistic pride
for the Cherokee Nation in Indian Territory. Still, the preference of
these Cherokee educators for English language instruction and their
de-emphasis of "tribal traditions" in social studies curricula highlighted
both their socioeconomic and racial prejudices and their desire to train
Cherokee children so they could not be mistaken for "savage Indians"
or lumped in the same educational category as "Negroes."[20]

Still, the Cherokee language was not consigned to a slow death: it
was read in Cherokee newspapers and could be heard on the streets of
Tahlequah and in the common schools and seminaries where both teachers and students were bilingual.[21] What Cherokee leaders recognized by
the 1840s, however, was the fact that the vast majority of Cherokees lived
in diaspora. These leaders concluded that cultivating a sense of community and feelings of belonging for Cherokees relocated to Indian Territory
and scattered elsewhere throughout the United States required a system
of public education that would, as one former seminary pupil put it in
the 1930s, provide a means of transforming Cherokees "from savagery
among the wild Indians to our present great state we have today."[22]

Such statements reflected the degree to which the Cherokee
Nation's system of formal education, overseen by predominantly mixed-
race educators, tended to borrow from Euro-American conceptions of
racial evolution. It did so in ways that allowed Cherokees to emphasize
a narrative of historical "progress" among Cherokee people, an evolution from "savagery" to "civilization." Moreover, formal education in
a Cherokee institution enabled former pupils to exercise a degree of
control over the cultural flow of ideas about Native Americans, particularly the derogatory and racist ways in which indigenous people
were portrayed in American popular culture. In other words, a formal
education helped Cherokees to articulate a multifaceted Cherokee
identity, an identity that had the potential to disrupt the clichéd racial
categories that were common in late nineteenth- and early twentieth-
century America; educated Cherokees were empowered with language
malleable enough to give meaning to what had become a "multi-sited"
Cherokee identity (or identities).[23] However, as the following discussion demonstrates, the formal education that Cherokees received occurred not just in the classrooms and schoolhouses of the Cherokee
Nation; educational facilities operated by the U.S. government from
the Qualla Reservation in North Carolina to off-reservation boarding
schools in southern California all touched the lives of Cherokee children.[24] These educational experiences, especially those operated by
the U.S. government, gave rise to questions about the kind of "multi-
sited" Cherokee identity that could possibly emerge from institutions
characterized by oppressiveness and violence.

The founding of the Cherokee common schools in 1841, the Cherokee male and female seminaries in 1851 and 1857, respectively, and the establishment of the Cherokee Orphan Asylum in 1871 were designed to cultivate both attachment to the idea of the Cherokee Nation as a self-governing body politic and to make that civic community economically prosperous.[25] These formal institutions of education collectively owned and operated by the Cherokee people were not simply a source for instilling nationalistic pride and training civically engaged Cherokee citizens; they constituted tangible institutional "chords" that both inspired and united what had become a new political homeland for the Cherokee diaspora.

Cherokee leaders viewed these educational institutions as vital to declaring to the outside world their sovereignty and territorial attachment to a new political homeland in diaspora. Article VI, Section IX of the Cherokee Constitution (1839) outlined just how important educational institutions were for the Cherokees: "Religion, morality, and knowledge being necessary to good government, the preservation of liberty and happiness of mankind, schools and the means of education shall forever be encouraged in this nation."[26] By the 1880s, the heyday for public education in the Cherokee Nation in Indian Territory, 106 day schools educated 1,704 boys and 1,308 girls. By the turn of the century, these schools numbered 124 and formed part of a rigorous education system that also included an orphanage, three boarding schools, four mission schools, and four academies.[27]

The male and female seminaries were the crown jewels of the Cherokee Nation's education system. From these seminaries, students sometimes went on to pursue further education in the United States, and seminary students often took on leading roles in the civic life of the Cherokee Nation.[28] The Cherokee Male Seminary, for example, was deemed to be so important to the future of the Cherokee people that it had the distinction of being the first nonsectarian public institution of higher learning established in the trans-Mississippi West. It educated future political leaders, lawyers, and bankers.[29] In contrast, the Female Seminary was modeled after the system of education offered to young ladies at Mount Holyoke Seminary in Massachusetts, and taught women gender-specific skills such as needlework and the "domestic arts."[30] Such skills would ensure that future generations of Cherokee mothers would oversee well-run households and ensure that their own children were taught pride in, and loyalty for, the Cherokee Nation in Indian Territory.

The female and male seminaries served the higher education needs of young Cherokee women and men until 1909, when the state

Figure 1. The Cherokee Female Seminary, Library of Congress Prints and Photographs Division, Washington, D.C., HABS OKLA, 11-TAHL, 1A—1.

of Oklahoma converted the female seminary into the Northeastern State Normal School, and 1910, when fire destroyed the male seminary for the second and final time.[31] During the institutions' life spans, students came from the various districts of the Cherokee Nation and from throughout the diaspora. George Candy, for example, attended the male seminary after receiving his initial education from the Baptist mission at Tahlequah. Candy's family background reflected the complex migration histories of Cherokee seminarians. Candy was known as a "full-blood," but his two sisters were considered "half-blood" and "three-quarter-blood" Cherokee, respectively. In explaining his family's confusing genealogy, Candy claimed that while his father was considered by community members to be a "full-blood" Cherokee, his mother was a "Digger Indian" from California, and the original Candy family patriarchs were English. Candy had no rational explanation for how his father acquired his Cherokee identity, admitting, "I do not know how my father came to be a full-blood."[32]

Former students like George Candy reflect on how the student body of the male and female seminaries also mirrored the class divisions in Cherokee society and the genealogical complexity that characterized the Cherokee diaspora. Children from prominent Cherokee families—such as the Adair, Ross, Bushyhead, Hicks, and Thompson families—retained a virtually constant connection with the seminaries. The presence of students and teachers from leading Cherokee families, many of them "mixed-blood" or with marital connections to white America, underscored the racially and ethnically complex nature of Cherokee class divisions by the latter third of the nineteenth century. Devon Mihesuah, one of the leading historians of Cherokee education, argues that tensions between so-called "progressive mixed-bloods" and students from "traditional" backgrounds led to a perpetually tense atmosphere at the female seminary. As Mihesuah explains, "some students were fullbloods, while others were blond, blue-eyed women of only 1/128 Cherokee blood."[33] In special circumstances, seminary staff did in fact admit white students. For example, the sons of the Moravian minister T. M. Rights—Lewis, Eugene, and Herbert—were admitted to the male seminary and graduated from that institution in the late 1880s. And Florence Caleb, a white student, graduated from the female seminary in 1885.[34] These students were exceptions; more typically, the blond-haired, blue-eyed students were in fact mixed-race Cherokee children, some of whom went on to become skilled professionals, teachers, politicians, judges, and lawyers, while others took advantage of oil, timber, and coal resources located on Cherokee land and accumulated great personal wealth in the process.[35]

The accumulation of individual wealth among a handful of former seminarians lay in the future, however. In the late nineteenth century, one of the central concerns of seminary educators was how to reignite feelings of loyalty and devotion to a common sense of Cherokee identity. Educators emphasized how "life is duty" and "God is love," messages repeated in song, literature, and daily lessons.[36] When the female seminary reopened after the Civil War in 1872, the racial and class prejudices of prominent Cherokee families with links to the seminaries persisted.[37] Disdain for "full-blood" traditionalists was one thread that continued to help some Cherokees define their identity. However, after the war such prejudices came under fire from disgruntled parents, especially those of students from poorer or culturally "traditional" backgrounds. The admission of these so-called traditional students to the male and female seminaries exposed the discriminatory racial and class views that shaped not only seminary culture, but Cherokee life more generally. This dynamic within the seminaries, and in the daily life of the Cherokee Nation outside of the seminary campus, could be identified in how mixed-race students and teachers viewed Cherokee-speaking "full-blood" students as "a little bit backward," while Cherokee leaders voiced that reviving "traditional" Cherokee cultures would be unhelpful in the racially charged fight against allotment and the dissolution of the Cherokee Nation's sovereignty.[38]

Another layer of racial tension in the Cherokee Nation's education institutions involved antiblack prejudice. Children of freedpeople were generally confined to the "Negro High School" and a few public schools. These segregationist practices helped to naturalize perceptions of black people as not legitimately entitled to Cherokee citizenship, or any degree of social and economic equality in the Cherokee Nation.[39]

The segregation of Cherokee freedmen—and African Americans generally—in the late nineteenth-century Cherokee Nation had its origins in the Cherokee adoption of racial slavery in the Southeast in the eighteenth and nineteenth centuries. When removal came to the Cherokee Nation in the 1830s, many slaveholding Cherokee families took their slaves with them to Indian Territory. These enslaved people helped he bring prosperity to the Cherokee Nation in Indian Territory, but when the Civil War reached the trans-Mississippi, thousands of slaves seized the moment, fled plantations in Indian Territory and throughout the trans-Mississippi region, and hoped that a new dawn of freedom would be theirs once the war ended. That freedom came when the Cherokee Nation, which sided with the Confederate States during the Civil War, came to terms with the U.S. government in 1866, in a treaty that stipulated the conditions under which former slaves could legally claim citizenship in the Cherokee Nation in Indian Territory.[40]

The abolition of slavery, however, did not mean an end to racial prejudice in the Cherokee Nation. Antiblack sentiment was not hard to find in the Cherokee Nation during the late nineteenth century, and the nation's educational facilities were among the most prominent institutions to reflect this racism. As Devon Mihesuah argues, the "separation of the red and black races at the behest of the Cherokees demonstrated that many Cherokees—traditionalists and progressives alike—needed to prove their superiority over blacks in order to keep from being lumped into the category of 'people of color' along with the former slaves."[41]

During the late 1860s and early 1870s, the educational challenges facing Cherokee leaders were bigger than issues of racial segregation and the desire—conscious or not—to cultivate in Cherokee children a "progressive" identity that differentiated "modern" Cherokees from "full-blood traditionalists" or people of African descent. If the forced removals of the late 1830s had not already alerted Cherokee leaders to the fraying of kin networks, then the refugee crisis and the alarming rise in the orphan population after the American Civil War surely did. Cherokee leaders like William Adair Duncan believed that raising orphaned Cherokee children as part of the civic and economic life of the Cherokee Nation was of utmost importance.

Cherokee efforts to establish an orphanage began in the 1850s. However, it was not until 1871 that the Cherokee Orphan Asylum was finally founded.[42] Before this, Cherokee orphans were cared for and educated in the Cherokee Nation's public school system—a system far more rigorous and comprehensive that many school systems in the United States, especially in the South.[43]

William Duncan was the most vocal advocate for the establishment of the orphan asylum. After spending the Civil War years in Texas, he returned to the Cherokee Nation and became disturbed by the number of orphans in the Cherokee Nation.[44] Due to Duncan's activism on behalf of the Cherokee orphans, the National Council agreed to finance a facility dedicated to their care and education. The "inmates," as they were referred to, were categorized as orphans, who were usually children who had lost both parents due to death; "half-orphans," whose family had suffered the loss of one parent; destitute children, or children from families unable to support a child or children; abandoned youths; and "orphans of Indian descent" who were not Cherokee, but whose tribal nation was willing to pay for their maintenance.[45] Educators at the orphanage placed "inmates" in one of three departments: the high school; the common school; or the intermediate and primary school. Progression through these three levels was designed to prepare individuals for further education, often at the Cherokee male or female seminary, and an adult life defined by "usefulness" to the Cherokee Nation and loyalty to ideals associated with Cherokee citizenship.[46]

The plan for the Cherokee Orphan Asylum and its inmates was simple: a basic education that equipped individuals with English literacy and accommodations that were cheap yet comfortable. As a "Native" explained in an open letter to the editor of the *Cherokee Advocate* on June 6, 1874, the "full-blood children who have been admitted . . . have all acquired the English language sufficiently in one years time, to speak it and think in it." The writer insisted that this type of education prepared students for a life as honest, working-class people. Training in agriculture was deemed an especially important supplement to a rudimentary education in English literacy. As the "Native" declared, "This is the plan that our leading men favor for our full-blood children. Cheap, comfortable buildings on the plan of old Dwight Mission, with a good farm, is what we deem necessary."[47]

By the late 1880s and 1890s, Cherokee leaders remained committed to the nation's orphanage as Euro-Americans made increasingly aggressive claims on Cherokee communal landholdings, and the federal government moved toward dismantling indigenous political sovereignty. The nation, Principal Chief S. H. Mayes declared in 1895, was the basis upon which a common Cherokee kinship must be focused. Cherokees could live throughout the nation, the trans-Mississippi West, or anywhere in diaspora for that matter, but the Cherokee Nation in Indian Territory must persist as a political homeland and a potential territorial refuge for Cherokees everywhere. Critical to such a vision were educational facilities that met the needs of the most vulnerable (orphans) and the most talented (seminary students). As Mayes described the role of education in nurturing national kinship among "our parentless children," the "educational interests of every country merit at all times the patriotic and devoted attention of the legislative branch of the government."[48]

The Cherokee were proud of their high levels of educational attainment and literacy. Such accomplishments, William P. Ross often insisted, reflected how the "Cherokee are not just progressive, they are *rapidly* progressive, and self-sustaining." Indeed, Ross instructed Cherokees to "keep your faith. But few Indians are left. Those, in Indian Territory, are quiet, peaceable, progressive, and friendly." Ross asserted the Cherokee people's racial equality and common interests with white Americans, insisting that the federal government should protect the Cherokee Nation and prevent its "extermination" because "in the course of a few years, they may imperceptibly be mingled in blood, sentiment, intelligence, and high aspirations with your own descendants."[49]

The existence of Cherokee orphans, however, highlighted just how serious the various social, political, and military pressures being placed on the Cherokee people were. For over a century, these pressures had steadily dispersed the Cherokee people across North America, fragmenting kinship networks in the process. This is not to say that Cherokee kinship and a sense of communal belonging were erased; they were not.[50] Instead, Cherokee leaders recognized that they had to reimagine kin and community bonds They had an important role to play during an uncertain era in Cherokee history to develop strategies that would educate and find "a home for the homeless."[51] For example, Martha A. Stewart, writing to the Cherokee National Council from Louisiana in 1893, requested assistance for her orphaned grandson. Stewart claimed that her parents were "one fourth Cherokee by blood," and thus she was entitled to place her grandson in the care of the Cherokee Orphan Asylum. To prove that she was not an opportunistic southern white woman preying on the compassion of the Cherokee Nation, Stewart insisted that her adult children were making their own way in the world but that her orphan grandson required the type of care and education that only the orphanage could provide.[52]

Graduates of the Cherokee Orphan Asylum remained proud of the education they received. Robert Choate, for example, became a successful farmer and active in Republican Party politics. Choate claimed that he was descended from "old settlers," or those Cherokees who comprised the vanguard of the Cherokee diaspora in the Arkansas Valley during the late eighteenth and early nineteenth centuries. He also insisted that he was a "3/8 blood" Cherokee, and "proud of that fact." It should not come as a surprise, then, that Choate took pleasure in recalling how he was cared for and educated at the Cherokee Orphan Asylum.[53]

As the nineteenth century neared its close, political pressures for the dissolution of the Cherokee Nation grew, and Oklahoma statehood became more imminent, Cherokee leaders remained determined to keep the orphan asylum in their control. It was an institutional jewel they jealously protected. However, their commitment to the asylum was tested in 1903 when fire destroyed the asylum building. Temporary housing for the orphans was provided at the Whittaker Asylum, before Cherokee leaders made the decision to convert the Cherokee Indian Asylum into an orphanage.[54] But allotment and the dismantling of Cherokee sovereignty did eventually come to the Cherokee diaspora's political homeland in Indian Territory. When it did, the federal government closed many Cherokee public schools, severely limiting the educational opportunities for Cherokees in the former nation. The orphan asylum, though, remained open. When federal officials assumed responsibilities for the asylum, they introduced strict codes of punishment, including corporeal punishment for failure to speak English, and the Bureau of Indian Affairs' "outing" system, which placed inmates in the employment of whites over the summer months.[55]

Many Cherokees expressed their frustrations over the allotment process and the federal government's gutting of the Cherokee education system. These complaints increased in volume during the early twentieth century. In a letter to the editor of the *Orphan News*, one Cherokee correspondent lamented the manner in which the federal government had failed Cherokee children and called for a "Drift back . . . to our old time Cherokee statesman and see what they had to do with this Cherokee orphan school."[56] However, for most Cherokees the damage had been done.

**BOARDING SCHOOLS
AND CHEROKEE CHILDREN:
FROM NORTH CAROLINA TO CALIFORNIA**

In the Great Smoky Mountains, the federal government exercised great control over the education of Cherokee children during the early twentieth century. Just a few short years before the passage of the Indian Reorganization Act (1934), the federal government completed a census of the Eastern Band of Cherokees. Officials hoped to use data from the census to devise policies to improve the quality of life for Cherokees. Of particular concern to federal officials was the state of formal education among Eastern Band Cherokees in North Carolina.

The 1931 census of the Eastern Band found 3,192 "entirely self-supporting" North Carolina Cherokees living at the Qualla Boundary reservation—which, by the 1930s, included parts of Jackson, Graham, and Cherokee Counties, in addition to the "Cherokee heartland" in Swain County.[57] Of this population, 2,357 were designated "mixed-blood," with a mere 842 "full-bloods" remaining at the Qualla Boundary reservation.[58]

In general terms, scholars have identified three demographic groups among early twentieth-century Eastern Band Cherokees. The first, the "conservatives," or "traditionalists," are usually associated with a "full-blood" status. The second group consisted of the so-called "progressives," or individuals who adopted some aspects of white American culture. The third group was the "rural white Indians," typically white men who married Cherokee women. By the 1940s, a fourth group began emerging. Anthropologist Robert Thomas (Cherokee) referred to this group as "a new middle class," an upwardly mobile class who urged early twentieth-century tribal members to leave the "comforting cocoon of tribalism" behind them and nurture a culture that embodied the best qualities of Cherokee and Euro-American socioeconomic life.[59]

As these demographic groups jockeyed for political influence at the Qualla reservation, efforts to stamp out illiteracy and poverty intensified. Early twentieth-century tribal leaders believed that the people they represented were not prepared for the social and economic challenges that twentieth-century America posed. Some tribal leaders pointed to the so-called "remnant Cherokees" in Georgia, Tennessee, Alabama, and Virginia as examples of how to successfully equip one's self with the skills needed to navigate modern American life. The solution to the economic hardships and apparent cultural backwardness of the North Carolina Cherokees, then, was education.[60]

Educational efforts among Eastern Band Cherokees had been accelerating since the conclusion of the Civil War in 1865.[61] For example, the Hampton Normal and Agricultural Institute, founded by General Samuel Armstrong in Virginia in 1868, had a number of Cherokees among its Native American student body. In 1890, six Cherokees attended Hampton Institute, a figure that increased to twenty-five students six years later. Lottie Smith, the daughter of the principal chief of the Eastern Band, Nimrod Smith, attended Hampton in the late 1880s. There she endeared herself to staff with her musical talents and "a sweet voice" that reportedly entranced listeners.[62] Lottie was a success story, and students like her convinced white educators that all Cherokees in North Carolina must surely want to avail themselves of an education at Hampton. Hollis B. Frissell, who assumed General Armstrong's duties at Hampton in 1893, declared, "The 1,500 Cherokees of North Carolina are a hopeful tribe . . . Their reservation is near the school, and it seems eminently proper that Hampton should help them."[63]

In Eastern Band communities, education was traditionally an informal affair, with elders having the responsibility of preparing and educating children for adulthood. It was not until 1877 that an attempt was made to bring formal education to the North Carolina Cherokees. Dr. J. D. Garner, a Quaker from Tennessee, borrowed from the lessons of the early nineteenth century and implemented a version of the prevailing assimilationist ideals popular among the white educators of Native American children. Dr. Garner thus took two Cherokee boys and placed them in a school in Maryville, Tennessee. Garner hoped

Figure 2. Indian School, Cherokee, North Carolina, Library of Congress
Prints and Photographs Division, Washington, D.C., LC-USZ62-122837.

that when they returned to North Carolina as educated young men they would teach Cherokee children the lessons that they had received at Maryville.

During the 1880s and 1890s, the Quakers were at the forefront of efforts to bring a system of education to the North Carolina Cherokees. This system of education was designed to give Cherokee children the "opportunity" to assimilate into modern American society; Quaker educators had next to no interest in nurturing a unique Cherokee identity. As was the case with Richard Henry Pratt's plan for educating Native American children at the Carlisle Indian Industrial School in Pennsylvania and other off-reservation boarding schools, the Quakers envisioned a curriculum that taught basic literacy in English but was divided along gendered lines when it came to vocational training.[64] Boys, for example, were taught agricultural skills while Cherokee girls learned the "domestic arts," or "housekeeping," thus preparing them to become what Quaker educators imagined to be the ideal of a good housewife and mother. Above all else, Quaker teachers insisted that children receive instruction in "sound Christian morality." During the last two decades of the nineteenth century, Quaker missionaries established day schools at Cherokee, Echota Mission, Big Cove, Robbinsville, and Bird Town to advance their educational objectives.[65]

The Cherokee Boarding School was established in 1880. From 1892, white teachers, primarily Quakers, oversaw the school's daily operations, although the federal government controlled the school, as it did with other boarding schools throughout the United States. The teachers approached their task of educating Cherokee children with zeal. They insisted that the compulsory education of Cherokee children was essential to their future lest they "become as worthless as the young Negroes growing up among us without any education."[66]

The Cherokee Boarding School educated Eastern Band Cherokees, although students from other Indian tribes did attend the institution. Betty Mae Tiger Jumper, for example, a Seminole, graduated from the Cherokee Boarding School in 1945.[67] For the students who attended the Cherokee Boarding School in North Carolina, their memories of life within the institution were mixed. Some students, such as Henry Bradley, went on to become prominent members of the North Carolina Cherokee community. Bradley attended the Cherokee Boarding School at the turn of the century. Like a number of other promising Cherokees from North Carolina and from throughout the diaspora, he later enrolled at Carlisle.[68] After receiving his education, Bradley went on to serve in the United States Army during the First World War, spending much of the war along the Mexican–United States border. Once the war ended, he returned to North Carolina and began a career in public service, first serving as a councilman for Painttown, and later becoming the chief of the Eastern Band of Cherokees.[69]

Former students of the Cherokee Boarding School also recalled the emotional and physical hardships that characterized boarding school life. Former students remembered how the school's curriculum attempted to eradicate the Cherokee language and undermine the Cherokee *gadugi*, or system of cooperative labor, in preference for individual employment. Such an education left many former students feeling isolated and detached from other members of the North Carolina Cherokee community. Raymond Kinsland remembered those feelings vividly; he also recalled the new friendships that students sometimes forged. As the manager of the Cherokee Boys Club, Kinsland's memories of corporal punishment—which included "paddling" a child's bare buttocks and inserting soap into a student's mouth for speaking

in Cherokee—were counterbalanced by recollections of friendships forged in the Boys Club.[70]

Cherokee women recalled a mixture of experiences at the Cherokee Boarding School. Girls received a gender-specific form of vocational training. They learned the "general duties of the housewife," in addition to being instructed in "plain sewing and other needlework."[71] Early twentieth-century philanthropists and reformers encouraged this type of curriculum, adding that instruction in basketry should be part of the curriculum that girls received at the Cherokee Boarding School because it exposed them to the value of producing goods for sale on the open market.[72]

The experiences of Eastern Band children at the Cherokee Boarding School bore striking similarities to the experiences of Cherokees at boarding schools operated by the BIA throughout the United States, from the Carlisle Indian Industrial School in Pennsylvania, the Haskell Indian Industrial Training School in Kansas, and the Wheelock Academy in Oklahoma, to name just three.[73] Far from these institutions being "jewels" that lined the "heart-strings" of Cherokee identity, such facilities took a dire emotional toll on many of the students who passed through them. These institutions fractured Native American identities by separating children from family and community in an effort to assimilate them into white society. This proved the case on the westernmost frontier of the Cherokee diaspora in the United States. At Riverside, California, one of these institutions was the Sherman Institute.

The Sherman Institute educated students from indigenous communities and mixed-race Native families from California, Arizona, New Mexico, Idaho, Oregon, Nevada, Oklahoma, Montana, Utah, South Dakota, Wisconsin, and Nebraska.[74] Like Carlisle, on which it was modeled, the Sherman Institute's mission was to assimilate Native children into the economic, social, and cultural life of white America. Sherman was the first off-reservation boarding school to open for Native American children in California. Originally founded in 1892 as the Perris Indian School in Perris, California, the school relocated to Riverside, California, where it enrolled its first students in September 1902 at the renamed Sherman Institute.[75] Perris/Sherman was one of twenty-four off-reservation boarding schools founded by the BIA between 1879 and 1900.[76] During the early twentieth century, the Sherman Institute continued to provide indigenous children with an education that emphasized practical skills and an adherence to Christian morality, and the school put in place a system known as "outing," in which students were placed with white families in order to gain practical work experience.[77] According to the National Education Association, the Sherman Institute provided students "not simply the lessons taught in books, but more valuable things—how to carry responsibility, how to take care of themselves, how to hold their own against the whites."[78]

Prior to the Second World War, forty-five children of Cherokee descent attended Sherman. These students came from towns and cities in California—such as Sacramento, Modesto, and Redding in northern California, Ontario, Los Angeles, and Anaheim in southern California—in addition to Oklahoma and Arizona. Official records indicate that Cherokee students possessed "blood quantum" ranging from "full-blood" to 1/32nd Cherokee blood. By far the most commonly recorded "blood quantum" was "one-quarter blood," with nineteen students categorized in this group. The recording of "blood-quantum," however, was not a simple matter of BIA officials assigning a racial designation to a child so they could determine a child's eligibility for enrollment at Sherman. Indeed, student case files indicate a subtle racial and cultural battle between federal officials and students. Federal government efforts to define a child's racial identity was matched by the determination of children and their families to stand firm in defending a child's self-perception of his or her indigeneity.

Student case files also provide clues as to how children of Cherokee descent came to be enrolled at a federally operated off-reservation boarding school in southern California. Since the gold rush era of the 1840s and 1850s, California had been a popular destination for Cherokees. For example, John Rollin Ridge, the son of the prominent early nineteenth-century Cherokee leader John Ridge, took refuge in northern California after he got into an argument with a man in Arkansas over a horse and murdered him. Other Cherokees sought gold and wealth; most left California disappointed. However, California did leave its mark on Cherokees. For example, those who returned to the Cherokee Nation in Indian Territory named a town in honor of the "golden state" in the late nineteenth century.[79]

California continued to attract Cherokees and mixed-race Cherokee families during the early twentieth century. Like hundreds of thousands of families who worked marginal and poor farming land in America's Dust Bowl, Oklahoman and Arkansas families of Cherokee descent felt the devastating effects of drought and the financial hardships in the decades after the Dawes Act.[80] Thus, John Price and other scholars of American demography claim that Cherokees were at the forefront of Native American migrations from Oklahoma to Arizona, Nevada, and especially California during the early twentieth century.[81] Demographic data makes this point clear. As Russell Thornton has shown, the Cherokee population in California grew from 258 in 1930 to 51,394 by 1980.[82]

There exist few explicit pieces of written evidence to ascertain how Cherokees in California understood their identities during the early twentieth century. The records of the Sherman Institute, however, provide brief historical snapshots into the lives of young Cherokees. Some children aspired for a better life, others struggled to define who they were in a predominantly white world, and still others found a sense of community and belonging elusive within the oppressive confines of a federal institution.

A number of the Cherokee students at Sherman appear to have set themselves lofty life goals, albeit in ways that conformed to the assimilationist ideals of Sherman's staff. Take, for example, Charles Starr. In 1927, Charles Starr entered the Sherman Institute and quickly distinguished himself as a model student. He excelled in both his academic and vocational studies, earning a reputation for being a brilliant public speaker. By 1932, Starr had endeared himself to students and staff alike and was elected "yell leader" of the Liberty Society, a student debate club. In the minds of Sherman's white educators, Starr had become a model of Indian assimilation.[83]

To Sherman Institute educators and BIA officials, a child like Starr was an ideal candidate for assimilation into American social and economic life. His father was classified by federal officials as "three-quarter blood" Cherokee; his mother was "one-quarter blood" Cherokee. While student records suggest that Starr classified himself as "half-blood Cherokee," officials enrolled him at Sherman as "three-eights Cherokee."[84] Perceived by Sherman enrollment officers as nearer to white than a "half-blood" Indian, Starr was therefore being "taken care of, taught, and drilled" so that he could eventually assimilate into white society.[85]

Taking light-skinned Cherokee children from family environments that BIA officials deemed unstable was a routine justification for enrollments at Sherman. Student case files indicate that a large percentage of Cherokee students were sent to Sherman Institute because their home life was reportedly characterized by impoverishment, a lack of adequate parental supervision, or juvenile delinquency.[86] Children like Elizabeth Hobbs, a "three-eighths" Cherokee from Sacramento, California, were seen as growing up in an impoverished family environment. Hobbs's parents separated in a bitter divorce, her white father leaving California and relocating to the East Coast. While Elizabeth's father did not want her to visit her mother on weekends, officials reported that Hobbs, who "is a blond and . . . looks white," had a "three-quarter blood" Cherokee mother who "is not one of the Indians that present a problem."[87] Sadly, no records survive that allow us to understand how Hobbs viewed her Cherokee identity. What we do know is that despite the ongoing feud between Elizabeth Hobbs's parents, she entered Sherman and performed moderately well.

BIA officials and educators at Sherman aimed to assimilate children like Elizabeth Hobbs into white society. In this objective, Sherman educators were supremely confident. However, the Sherman Institute's case files suggest that such optimism was often misplaced. Take for example the case of the Cherokee brothers Kay and Robert Beldon. According to Kay Beldon, he and his brother felt out of place at Sherman.

The Beldon case file presents a picture of two young men supremely unhappy with life at Sherman. Thus, in a letter to his mother on September 2, 1926, Kay Beldon expressed his intention to run away from Sherman. Shortly after that letter was mailed the Beldon brothers made good on their promise and absconded.

The Sherman Institute's superintendent, Frank Conser, expressed his willingness to "give the boys another chance" and accept the brothers back into the institute.[88] However, after the brothers fled once again, Robert Beldon Sr., the boys "half-blood" Cherokee father, was clearly angered by the misconduct of his sons. Writing to Superintendent Conser on September 21, 1926, Beldon Sr. instructed, "I want you to get the Boys Back [sic] and punish them so they won't repeat it again."[89] Beldon's wife, Hazel Wright, who was white, worried that her sons were not given the same consideration as female students. In fact, she complained that the authorities "dont [sic] take them back or make any effort to find them. When the girls run away they do try to get them."[90]

Hazel Wright's anxiety was justified. In 1929 her sons were refused reentry to Sherman.[91] The Beldon case was representative of how some Cherokee children from mixed race families found the educational environment at Sherman unsupportive and unproductive in fostering an enriching form of Cherokee identification. The Beldon brothers expressed feelings—in both their words and deeds—of being out of place in the rigid institutional environment offered by the BIA at boarding schools like Sherman. Appearing to make few friends among fellow students, and failing to endear themselves to BIA staff, their experiences with institutional education seem to have nurtured little more than anomie.

CONCLUSION

The trials and tribulations of Native Americans at boarding schools are well-known. Violence, both physical and emotional in nature, scarred many thousands of indigenous children as they entered the later stages of their lives. The case files from the Sherman Institute and the Cherokee Boarding School in North Carolina tend to reinforce this point. The white educators and officials in charge of these institutions showed little interest in strengthening the "heart-string" of "national kinship" among Cherokee children. Obsessed with assimilating indigenous children to white American society, white educators and missionaries worked actively to erode feelings of kinship toward the Cherokee Nation in Indian Territory or the Eastern Band in North Carolina. With the support of the federal government, educators and missionaries sought to sever linguistic, cultural, or any emotional connections to Cherokee identity. In essence, BIA boarding schools served a single purpose: to ethnically cleanse Native Americans from the United States.

This was the case for Cherokee children who attended the Sherman Institute. Located many thousands of miles from the Cherokee diaspora's political homeland in Indian Territory/Oklahoma, and from the ancient homeland occupied by Eastern Band Cherokees in the Great Smoky Mountains, Sherman's Cherokee students faced grave challenges in cultivating a meaningful sense of self or attachments to family and community. Some students, such as the Beldon brothers, appear to have experienced only alienation. Lacking any clearly acknowledged sense of belonging to a larger Cherokee community, and seeming to feel abandoned or isolated from family, too many boarding school children shared the Beldons' feelings of frustration and loss.[92]

In the Cherokee Nation in Indian Territory, though, the Cherokee system of public education was established to play a major role in cultivating both skilled young people and restoring bonds of national affection for a people exiled from their southeastern homeland in the trans-Mississippi West. Public education, as William Adair Duncan conceived of it, was indeed a "jeweled chord" that should bind young Cherokees together in feelings of national pride and a sense of collective belonging. These imagined heartstrings may at times fray, but so long as the Cherokee Nation retained its educational institutions, an abiding emotional connection to the Cherokee Nation was never beyond repair.

This brand of nationalistic education came at a cost, however. By the latter third of the nineteenth century, the Cherokee Nation in Indian Territory was a political homeland for a diasporic people descended from multiple overlapping diasporas—European, African, and Native American. The Cherokee Nation's education system failed to adequately nurture the beneficial qualities of many decades, indeed centuries, of racial and ethnic mixture. Instead, the Cherokee system of public education—especially its seminaries of higher learning—tended to reinforce popular prejudices. These prejudices, such as the contempt that "progressive" mixed-race Cherokees directed toward "full-blood" Cherokees, or the racially discriminatory views of Cherokee seminarians for people of African descent, reflected the limits of nationalistic forms of education and the entanglement of the Cherokee Nation's heartstrings with American nationalist (and racist) sentiment. Indeed, in appearing to share the racial, gendered, and linguistic prejudices common to late nineteenth- and early twentieth-century American nationalism, the Cherokee Nation's educational institutions not only reified popular prejudices, but they compromised the ability of the nation's leading citizens to coordinate a united defense against severalty and allotment. While an education system that was nationalistic in outlook had potential to unite diasporic Cherokees, the internal weaknesses in that system—its perpetuation of popular prejudices and its failure to adequately embrace a multiethnic, multilingual system of education—ultimately proved ineffective in meeting the challenges posed by the United States' brand of settler colonialism during the late nineteenth and early twentieth century.

AUTHOR BIOGRAPHY

Gregory D. Smithers is associate professor of history at Virginia Commonwealth University. His most recent book is *The Cherokee Diaspora: An Indigenous History of Migration, Resettlement, and Identity* (2015).

NOTES

1 Daniel F. Littlefield Jr. and James W. Parins, *A Bibliography of Native American Writers 1772–1924: A Supplement* (Metuchen, N.J.: Scarecrow Press, 1985), 204.

2 "Education: Cherokee Nation," Folder 6, Box 57, Federal Writers' Project, 81.105, Oklahoma Historical Society, Norman, Okla., [hereafter OHS] 2–3; Jon Reyhner and Jeanne Eder, *American Indian Education: A History* (Norman: University of Oklahoma Press, 2004), 55; Charles L. Glenn, *American Indian/First Nations Schooling: From the Colonial Period to the Present* (New York: Palgrave Macmillan, 2011), 42.

3 *Cherokee Orphan Asylum Press*, I, 17 (March 10, 1881), in Cherokee Orphan Asylum Press, 88.22, OHS.

4 Gregory D. Smithers, *The Cherokee Diaspora: An Indigenous History of Migration, Resettlement, and Identity* (New Haven, Conn.: Yale University Press, 2015).

5 Devon A. Mihesuah, *Cultivating the Rosebuds: The Education of Women at the Cherokee Female Seminary, 1851–1909* (Urbana: University of Illinois Press, 1998); Marilyn Irvin Holt, *Indian Orphanages* (Lawrence: University of Kansas Press, 2001).

6 *Cherokee Orphan Asylum Press*, I, 17 (March 10, 1881); Mark E. Miller, *Claiming Tribal Identity: The Five Tribes and the Politics of Federal Acknowl-edgment* (Norman: University of Oklahoma Press, 2013), 96; Glenn, *American Indian/First Nations Schooling*, 42.

7 "Education: Cherokee Nation," 4.

8 David Wallace Adams, *Education for Extinction: American Indians and the Boarding School Experience* (Lawrence: University of Kansas Press, 1995), 17–18; Matthew L. M. Fletcher, *American Indian Education: Counternarratives in Racism, Struggle, and the Law* (New York and London: Routledge, 2008), 4.

9 Adams, *Education for Extinction*, 97. For the ideologies driving assimilationist education, see also Gary Gerstle, *American Crucible: Race and Nation in the Twentieth Century* (Princeton, N.J.: Princeton University Press, 2001), 7–8.

10 Mary Young, "The Cherokee Nation: Mirror of the Republic," *American Quarterly* 33, no. 5 (Winter 1981): 502–24.

11 William McLoughlin, *Cherokee Renascence in the New Republic* (Princeton, N.J.: Princeton University Press, 1992); William McLoughlin, *After the Trail of Tears: The Cherokees' Struggle for Sovereignty, 1839–1880* (Chapel Hill: University of North Carolina Press, 1993); Andrew Denson, *Demanding the Cherokee Nation: Indian Autonomy and American Culture, 1830–1900* (Lincoln: University of Nebraska Press, 2004).

12 Cherokees encountered missionary educators during the eighteenth and early nineteenth centuries, and also attended prominent universities such as Princeton and Vanderbilt. S. S. Cobb, *Indian Pioneer Papers*, Western Historical Collections, University of Oklahoma, Norman, Vol. 18, January 27, 1938, 422 [hereafter *IPP*]; Oliver Hazard Perry Brewer Jr., *IPP*, Vol. 11, n.d., 125; Callie Losier, *IPP*, Vol. 55, 1938, 305; Chas G. Watts, *IPP*, Vol. 116, n.d., 541; "Life of Joshua Ross, Indian Pioneer, Given by Susie Ross Martin," *IPP*, Vol. 61, June 11, 1937, 5; Spencer Stephens, *IPP*, Vol. 87, n.d., 234–35; W. W. Hastings, *IPP*, Vol. 106, n.d., 185; Joseph Martin Lynch, *IPP*, Vol. 56, April 13, 1937, 302.

13 Sandy Grande, *Red Pedagogy: Native American Social and Political Thought* (Lanham, Md.: Rowman and Littlefield Publishers, Inc., 2004), 83.

14 Taloteske & Cunnetue to Return Meigs, June 23, 1810, Records of the Bureau of Indian Affairs, Records of the Cherokee Indian Agency, East, Record Group 75, 19, 8, National Archives and Records Administration (hereafter NARA), Washington, D.C.; Notes on Cherokee History, Vol. VI, John Howard Payne Papers, 1794–1841, Ayer Ms. 689, Newberry Library, Chicago [hereafter NL], 206–7; Sean Teuton, *Cherokee Stories of the Turtle Island Liars' Club: Dalaski elohi anigagoga junilawisdii (Turtle, earth, the liars, meeting place)* (Chapel Hill: University of North Carolina Press, 2012), 11.

15 *Cherokee Phoenix*, February 18, 1832, 1 [hereafter *CP*]; Russell Thornton, *The Cherokees: A Population History* (Lincoln: University of Nebraska Press, 1990), 68.

16 Rose Stremlau, *Sustaining the Cherokee Family: Kinship and the Allotment of an Indigenous Nation* (Chapel Hill: University of North Carolina Press, 2011), 119.

17 Ellen Cushman, *The Cherokee Syllabary: Writing the People's Perseverence* (Norman: University of Oklahoma Press, 2011); Lee Irwin, *Coming Down from Above: Prophecy, Resistance, and Renewal in Native American Religions* (Norman: University of Oklahoma Press, 2014), 207.

18 *Programs of Exercises. Female Seminary. Male Seminary & Teachers Institute*, Commencement, Cherokee National Seminaries, Week of June 21, 1896 (Tahlequah: Arrow Printing Company, 1896), in Box 1, T. L. Ballenger Papers, 1887–1936, 97.53, OHS; Mihesuah, *Cultivating the Rosebuds*, 22, 30, 80.

19 Carol L. Schmid, *The Politics of Language: Conflict, Identity, and Cultural Pluralism in Comparative Perspective* (New York: Oxford University Press, 2001), 23–24; Susan Tamasi and Lamont Antieau, *Language and Linguistic Diversity in the U.S.: An Introduction* (New York and Milton Park: Routledge, 2015), 258.

20 See "Cherokee Male Seminary" and "Cherokee Female Seminary" in "Education: Cherokee Nation," Folder 6, Box 57, Federal Writers' Project, 81.105, OHS; Mihesuah, *Cultivating the Rosebuds*, 56, 109.

21 Department of the Interior, *Extra Census Bulletin: The Five Civilized Tribes in Indian Territory* (Washington, D.C.: U.S. Census Printing Office, 1894), 13–14; Glenn, *American Indian/First Nations Schooling*, 42.

22 Josephine Pennington, *IPP*, Vol. 70, October 12, 1937, 358.

23 George E. Marcus, *Ethnography through Thick and Thin* (Princeton, N.J.: Princeton University Press, 1998), 79–86, 136.

24 Sally J. McBeth, *Ethnic Identity and the Boarding School Experience of West-Central Oklahoma American*

Indians (Washington, D.C.: University Press of America, 1983); K. Tsianina Lomawaima, *They Called It Prairie Light: The Story of Chilocco Indian School* (Lincoln: University of Nebraska Press, 1994); Adams, *Education for Extinction*; Clifford E. Trafzer, Jean A. Keller, and Lorene Sisquoc, eds., *Boarding School Blues: Revisiting American Indian Educational Experiences* (Lincoln: University of Nebraska Press, 2006); Jacqueline Fear-Segal, *White Man's Club: Schools, Race, and the Struggle of Indian Acculturation* (Lincoln: University of Nebraska Press, 2007).

25 Brad Agnew, "Legacy of Education: The History of the Cherokee Seminaries," *The Chronicles of Oklahoma* 63 (Summer 1985): 128–47; Mihesuah, *Cultivating the Rosebuds*, 1–2.

26 *The Constitution and Laws of the Cherokee Nation: Passed at Tahlequah, Cherokee Nation, 1839* (Washington, D.C.: Gale and Seaton, 1840), 15.

27 "Education: Cherokee Nation," Folder 6, Box 57, Federal Writers' Project. 81.105, OHS.

28 On seminary students going on to pursue education throughout the United States, see for example, Stephen Foreman to "Nannie," October 6, 1874, Folder 12, LETTERS of GB (Bullet) Foreman, OHS.

29 Devon Mihesuah, "Out of the 'Graves of the Polluted Debauches': The Boys of the Cherokee Male Seminary," *American Indian Quarterly* 15, no. 4 (Fall 1991): 503–5.

30 Andy A. Cordray, *IPP*, Vol. 20, 1938, 423; Annie Woodward, *IPP*, Vol. 100, Interviewed August 5, 1939, 233–35; Rod Richards, *IPP*, Vol. 75, November 9, 1937, 470; Mihesuah, *Cultivating the Rosebuds*, 4, 103; Katja May, *African Americans and Native Americans in the Creek and Cherokee Nations, 1830s–1920s: Collision and Collusion* (New York and London: Routledge, 1996), 209–12.

31 Samuel Pryor, *IPP*, Vol. 73, n.d., 224; Sallie E. Dick, *IPP*, Vol. 24, n.d., 258.

32 George T. Candy, *IPP*, Vol. 15, March 8, 1937, 290–91.

33 Eli H. Whitmire, *IPP*, Vol. 18, October 30, 1937, 138; Devon A. Mihesuah, "Too Dark to Be Angels: The Class System among the Cherokees at the Female Seminary," *American Indian Culture and Research Journal* 15, no. 1 (1991): 31.

34 Florence Caleb Smith, *IPP*, Vol. 84, n.d., 494; Elizabeth Ross, *IPP*, Vol. 108, n.d. 499–502.

35 Mai M. Smith, *IPP*, Vol. 85, May 21, 1937, 253–54; Stephen R. Lewis, *IPP*, Vol. 53, July 9, 1937, 500; Mary J. Stockton, *IPP*, Vol. 57, n.d., 182; L. G. Jennings, *IPP*, Vol. 48, 1937, 63; Susanna Adair Davis, *IPP*, Vol. 23, March 18, 1937, 377; Mihesuah, *Cultivating the Rosebuds*, 63.

36 See, for example, Programme of Commencement Exercises of the Park Hill Seminary, June 26, 1879, Park Hill Seminary, 90.75, OHS.

37 Mihesuah, *Cultivating the Rosebuds*, 56, 61–63.

38 Mihesuah, *Cultivating the Rosebuds*, 4, 49; Mihesuah, "Too Dark to Be Angels," 35.

39 Mihesuah, *Cultivating the Rosebuds*, 61–63, 81–86.

40 For further details about the history of slavery and antiblack racism among the Cherokee, see R. Halliburton Jr., *Red over Black: Black Slavery among the Cherokee Indians* (Westport, Conn.: Greenwood Press, 1977); Theda Perdue, *Slavery and the Evolution of Cherokee Society, 1540–1866* (Knoxville: University of Tennessee

Press, 1979); Patrick N. Minges, *Slavery in the Cherokee Nation: The Keetoowah Society and the Defining of a People, 1855–1867* (New York and London: Routledge, 2003); Tiya Miles, *Ties That Bind: The Story of an Afro-Cherokee Family in Slavery and Freedom* (Berkeley: University of California Press, 2005); Tiya Miles, *The House of Diamond Hill: A Cherokee Plantation Story* (Chapel Hill: University of North Carolina Press, 2010); Fay A. Yarbrough, *Race and the Cherokee Nation: Sovereignty in the Nineteenth Century* (Philadelphia: University of Pennslyvania Press, 2008); Barbara Krauthamer, *Black Slaves, Indian Masters: Slavery, Emancipation, and Citizenship in the Native American South* (Chapel Hill: University of North Carolina Press, 2013).

41 Mihesuah, *Cultivating the Rosebuds*, 83.

42 "Act for the creation of the Cherokee Orphan asylum, dated October 23, 1856," Folder 623, Roll 6, Cherokee Nation Papers, University of Oklahoma, Norman.

43 In 1847, the superintendent of public schools in the Cherokee Nation, James M. Payne, reported that 121 orphans were cared for in the nation's public schools. See James M. Payne to James McKissick, September 7, 1847, Folder 24, Item 1, Box 7, Foreman Collection, OHS.

44 Johnie Mae Duncan Korthank, *IPP*, Vol. 51, August 19, 1937, 392–97.

45 Cherokee Nation, *Constitution and Laws of the Cherokee Nation* (St. Louis, Mo.: R. & T. A. Ennis, 1875), 260–62; *Report of the Commissioner of Education for the Year 1875* (Washington, D.C.: Government Printing Office, 1876), 116; Emmet Starr, *History of the Cherokee Indians and Their Legends and Folklore* (Oklahoma City: The Warden Company, 1921), 246; Holt, *Indian Orphanages*, 86, 103.

46 Annual Report of Orphan Asylum, October 13, 1877, Folder 684, Roll 6, Cherokee Nation Papers. In 1880, twelve "colored" orphans were reportedly cared for at the Cherokee Orphan Asylum. May, *African Americans and Native*, 208.

47 *Cherokee Advocate*, June 6, 1874, Folder 19, Box 1, William Potter Ross Collection, Western Historical Collection, University of Oklahoma, Norman [hereafter WHC]. Charles Thompson to National Council, Folder 1, Box O-21, Oochalata (Charles Thompson) Collection, WHC.

48 First Annual Message of S. H. Mayes, November 21, 1895, Folder 26, Box M-50, S. H. Mayes Collection, WHC.

49 Speech of WP Ross, presented to the House Committee of Territories, reprinted in the *Cherokee Advocate*, February 21, 1874, Folder 14, Box 1, William Potter Ross Collection; *The Indian Chieftain*, November 17, 1898, Folder 10, Box M-51, Mayes Collection.

50 Holt, *Indian Orphanages*, 84; Stemlau, *Sustaining the Cherokee Family*.

51 James R. Carselowey, *IPP*, Vol. 102, 416–18.

52 Martha A. Stewart to the National Council, February 1, 1893, Folder 16, Box H-55, C. Johnson Harris Collection, WHC.

53 Robert B. Choate, *IPP*, Vol. 18, March 19, 1937, 35–36.

54 Holt, *Indian Orphanages*, 108–11.

55 Ibid., 114.

56 *Orphans News*, December 26, 1891, quoted in Folder 15, Item 2, Box 5, Foreman Collection.

57 John Finger, *Cherokee Americans: The Eastern Band of Cherokees in the*

Twentieth Century (Lincoln: University of Nebraska Press, 1991), 55.

58 L. W. Page, "Census of the Eastern Cherokee Tribe of the Eastern Cherokee Reservation of the Cherokees, N.C. Jurisdiction, as of April 1, 1931," Item 1, Folder 10, Box 6, Foreman Collection, 1900–1956, 83.229, OHS.

59 Robert K. Thomas, "Eastern Cherokee Acculturation," Institute for Research in Social Sciences, Cross-Cultural Laboratory (Chapel Hill: University of North Carolina, 1958), 12–17. For the "comforting cocoon of tribalism," see Finger, *Cherokee Americans*, 53. See also John Gulick, *Cherokees at the Crossroads* (Chapel Hill: University of North Carolina Press, 1960), 128–46; Finger, *Cherokee Americans*, 66–67.

60 Finger, *Cherokee Americans*, 12, 73; Sharlotte Neely, *Snowbird Cherokees: People of Persistence* (Athens: University of Georgia Press, 1991), 28–30.

61 George E. Tinker, *Missionary Conquest: The Gospel and Native American Cultural Genocide* (Minneapolis, Minn.: Augsburg Fortress, 1993).

62 Virginia Moore Carney, *Eastern Band Cherokee Women: Cultural Persistence in their Letters and Speeches* (Knoxville: University of Tennessee Press, 2005), 86.

63 Donal F. Lindsay, *Indians at Hampton Institute, 1877–1923* (Urbana: University of Illinois Press, 1995), 203.

64 Ruth Spack, *America's Second Tongue: American Indian Education and the Ownership of English, 1860–1900* (Lincoln: University of Nebraska Press, 2002), 39.

65 Thomas Donaldson, *Eastern Band of Cherokees of North Carolina* (Washington, D.C.: U.S. Census Printing Office, 1892), 9; Sharlotte Neely, "The Quaker Era of Cherokee Indian Education, 1880–1892," *Appalachian Journal* 2, no. 4 (Summer 1975): 316–18.

66 Finger, *Cherokee Americans*, n35, 194–95.

67 Gretchen M. Bataille and Laurie Lisa, eds., *Native American Women: A Biographical Dictionary* (New York and London: Routledge, 2005), 227. Indigenous children from Virginia also attended the Cherokee Boarding School during the 1940s. See Helen C. Roundtree, *Pocahontas's People: The Powhatan Indians of Virginia through Four Centuries* (Norman: University of Oklahoma Press, 1990), 236.

68 *The Carlisle Arrow*, October 25, 1912, 4; *The Carlisle Arrow*, February 6, 1914, 8; *The Carlisle Arrow*, March 6, 1914, 2; John R. Finger, *The Eastern Band of Cherokees, 1819–1900* (Knoxville: University of Tennessee Press, 1984), 162, 169, 178; Finger, *Cherokee Americans*, 28; Genevieve Bell, "Telling Stories out of School: Remembering the Carlisle Indian Industrial School, 1879–1918" (PhD diss., Stanford University, 1998), 187; Carney, *Eastern Band Cherokee Women*, 193. The most famous Eastern Cherokee to attend Carlisle was also purported to be an imposter. Sylvester Long Lance, who went on to a career as a writer and actor, was in later life accused of not having the indigenous heritage he claimed to possess. See William T. Hagan, "Full Blood, Mixed Blood, and Erasatz: The Problem of Indian Identity," *Arizona and the West* 27, no. 4 (Winter 1995): 309–26.

69 Robert J. Conley, *A Cherokee Encyclopedia* (Albuquerque: University of New Mexico Press, 2007), 38.

70 Tamrala G. Swafford, "The *Gadu:Gi* Spirit: Community Development Strategies among the Eastern Band of Cherokee Indians, 1934 to 1984" (PhD diss.,

Arizona State University, 2009), 87. See, similarly, Barbara R. Duncan, ed., *Living Stories of the Cherokee* (Chapel Hill: University of North Carolina Press, 1998), 143. After the Second World War, the North Carolina Cherokees introduced Cherokee language immersion curricula to ensure that the Cherokee language did not become extinct. See Margaret C. Bender, *Signs of Cherokee Culture: Sequoyah's Syllabary in Eastern Cherokee Life* (Chapel Hill: University of North Carolina Press, 2002), 18.

71 *Eastern Band of Cherokees of North Carolina* (Washington, D.C.: United States Printing Office, 1892), 16.

72 Sarah H. Hill, "Marketing Traditions: Cherokee Basketry and Tourist Economies," in *Selling the Indian: Commercializing and Appropriating American Indian Cultures*, eds. Carter J. Meyer and Diana Royer (Tucson: University of Arizona Press, 2001), 217–18.

73 Michael C. Coleman, *American Indian Children at School, 1850–1930* (Jackson: University of Mississippi Press, 1993); Brenda J. Child, *Boarding School Seasons: American Indian Families, 1900–1940* (Lincoln: University of Nebraska Press, 2000); Fear-Segal, *White Man's Club.*

74 Records of the Bureau of Indian Affairs, Annual Reports (1912), Box 6, NARA, Laguna Niguel, Calif., 1; Records of the Bureau of Indian Affairs, Annual Reports (1917), Box 5, Ibid., 1, 4; Records of the Bureau of Indian Affairs, Annual Reports (1922), Box 5, Ibid., 1.

75 *Sherman Institute: U.S. Indian School, Riverside, California* (n.p., 1909), 1; Clifford E. Trafzer and Leleua Loupe, "From Perris Indian School to Sherman Institute," in *The Indian School on Magnolia Avenue:*

Voices and Images from Sherman Institute, eds. Clifford E. Trafzer, Matthew Sakiestewa Gilbert, and Lorene Sisquoc (Corvallis: Oregon State University Press), 19–34.

76 Adams, *Education for Extinction,* 58; Richard Henry Pratt, *Battlefield and Classroom: An Autobiography* (Norman: University of Oklahoma Press, 2003), xii.

77 Alice Littlefield, "The BIA Boarding School," *Humanity & Society* 13 (1989): 428–41; Donald L. Fixico, *Daily Life of Native Americans in the Twentieth Century* (Westport, Conn.: Greenwood Press, 2006), 48.

78 *Journal of Proceedings and Addresses of the Forty-Fifth Annual Meeting Held at Los Angeles, California, July 8–12, 1907* (Winona, Minn.: National Education Association, 1907), 1015.

79 James W. Parins, *John Rollin Ridge: His Life and Works* (Lincoln: University of Nebraska Press, 1991), 55; Starr, *History of the Cherokee Indians,* 665.

80 Walter J. Stein, *California and the Dust Bowl Migration* (Westport, Conn.: Greenwood Press, 1973), 145–47. See also James N. Gregory, *American Exodus: The Dust Bowl Migration and Okie Culture in California* (New York: Oxford University Press, 1991), 4.

81 John Price, "The Migration and Adaptation of American Indians to Los Angeles," *Human Organization* 27 (1968): 169.

82 Thornton, *The Cherokees,* 147–48.

83 Charles Starr, Central Classified Files, 1907–1939, Box 343, and Records of the Superintendent, Central Classified Files, 1907–1939, Sherman Institute, Annual Reports (1926), Box 7, NARA, Laguna Niguel, Calif.

84   Charles Starr, Records of the Superintendent, Central Classified Files, 1907–1939, Box 343, Sherman Institute.

85   *Reports of the U.S. Department of the Interior for the Fiscal Year Ended June 30, 1916*, Volume II (Washington, D.C.: Government Printing Office, 1917), 354.

86   David J. Wishart, *An Unspeakable Sadness: The Dispossession of the Nebraska Indians* (Lincoln: University of Nebraska Press, 1995), 96.

87   Elizabeth Hobbs, Student Case Files, 1903–1939, Box 151, Sherman Institute.

88   Superintendent Conser, August 13, 1926, Robert Cliffton Beldon, Student Case Files, 1903–1939, Box 31, Sherman Institute. See similarly Child, *Boarding School Seasons*, 87–95.

89   Robert Beldon Sr. to Superintendent Conser, September 21, 1926, Robert Cliffton Beldon, Student Case Files, 1903–1939, Box 31, Sherman Institute.

90   Hazel Wright to Robert Beldon Sr., September 14, 1926, Robert Cliffton Beldon, Student Case Files, 1903–1939, Box 31, Sherman Institute.

91   Robert E. Johnson to Superintendent Conser, February 12, 1929, Robert Cliffton Beldon, Student Case Files, 1903–1939, Box 31, Sherman Institute.

92   On this point, see Trafzer, Keller, and Sisquoc, *Boarding School Blues*.

Outside the Rules
Invisible American Indians in New York State

Samuel W. Rose and Richard A. Rose

Discussions and histories of American Indian peoples in New York State in popular culture (and even sometimes in academia) generally begin and often end with a review of the long and varied history of the Haudenosaunee (also known as the Five Nations or the Iroquois). This can be viewed as creating a distorted narrative that serves to essentially equate American Indian history in New York with Iroquois history. However, this idea is highly problematic in at least two major ways. For one, Iroquois peoples, both historically and contemporarily, are not bound simply to New York, as there are Iroquois people living on and off reservations in several states and Canadian provinces. Secondly, there are other indigenous populations that have lived and continue to live in New York, although their histories are less known.

After the relocation of much, but arguably not all, of the Tuscarora in the early eighteenth century from the Carolinas to New York, the Haudenosaunee became the Six Nations. Even this name is less than accurate, as by this time there were other American Indian populations that had moved into Central New York and had varying degrees of alliance and partnership with the Iroquois, including Stockbridge-Munsees, Brothertown Indians, and Mahicans (though these groups would be relocated westward to Wisconsin).[1] It is important to acknowledge that there are those Iroquois and Algonquin peoples who, while historically residing in New York State, currently reside in Canada, Oklahoma, Wisconsin, or elsewhere. The turmoil of the American Revolution

WICAZO SA REVIEW FALL 2015

and the subsequent state engineered land transfers of the nineteenth century, combined with larger U.S. national policies of Americanization and forced relocation,[2] resulted in Iroquois history taking on the character of a story involving multiple countries, multiple states, and multiple tribal governments. If this were the entire story of American Indian peoples in New York, this alone would be a fascinating and compelling story worthy of both academic and policy study.

However, there are many other stories of American Indians in New York State, outside of the greater Iroquois Confederacy, that have existed in scattered and obscure references in academic literature, and in all but forgotten community and family histories. Therefore, one purpose of this essay is to bring together much of this information so that these generally invisible, obscured, or forgotten American Indian peoples still living in New York may be part of the larger dialogue of indigenous people in North America. Through an examination of the academic literature we will try to showcase what indigenous populations are known to have existed in New York in the twentieth century (and may still exist in some form) in addition to the federally recognized tribes of the Haudenosaunee (Saint Regis Mohawk, Seneca Nation of Indians, Tonawanda Band of Seneca, Onondaga Nation, Cayuga Nation, Oneida Nation of New York, and Tuscarora Nation), the recently federally recognized Shinnecock Indian Nation, and the state-recognized Unkechaug Nation. The goal here is not simply to explore the commonly known populations, but also to examine those indigenous people whose tribal identity, tribal rights, and right to a future as an indigenous people have so far been withheld or forgotten, or whose status is either ambiguous or indefinite. We will also discuss how the notion of race and of racial purity contributed to the nonrecognition and delegitimization of certain populations as American Indian by outsiders, including government bureaucrats and scholars. While this review may not be exhaustive, it does serve to bring back into the discussion of indigenous people in New York those communities that for so many years have existed outside of mainstream discourse and outside of the existing colonial legal structure and its processes of recognition (and thus in our view exist "outside the rules").

This article places a particular focus on the role that scholars have in shaping indigenous identity. While indigenous identity is commonly understood in the United States and in other settler colonial nation-states to be shaped and policed by governmental policy, the role that scholars have had in shaping and informing the intellectual basis and rationale for settler colonial policy is less widely acknowledged. As such, scholars have often had a necessary functional role in providing the intellectual cover for colonial policies of dispossession and domination. This also raises several important issues for modern scholars working in the general field of indigenous studies. First, given this historical position that academia has had in the colonial structure, how can this role be changed? Second, to whom should scholarly productions be accountable? And third, how are counterhegemonic studies and discussions of indigenous identity to be conducted? In essence, this article emphasizes the position of the scholar on matters of indigenous identity and recognition because, in light of the role of scholars in producing the intellectual framework for colonial policies, it is hoped that an erosion of that intellectual framework by scholars and the production of new perspectives on and understandings of indigeneity will result in potential changes in federal Indian policy, the weakening and erosion of racialized understandings of indigeneity, and an increased social recognition of all types of indigenous communities.

IROQUOIS

When one reviews the historical interactions between New York State and the American Indian nations, it is possible to see that "New York State government, with few exceptions, has largely ignored native populations," especially in the era after legal domination failed.[3] It is also possible to see that from the earliest interactions between the Iroquois and the colonial powers the Iroquois have maintained their position as distinct and not under the jurisdiction of either the colonial governors or the succeeding governors after the creation of the state of New York. The New York State Assembly's *Report of Special Committee to Investigate the Indian Problem of the State of New York, 1889,* or the Whipple report, goes into great detail about the efforts undertaken to remove all American Indians from New York, even acknowledging that the process was not consistent with ethical legal procedures.[4]

In 1944, while facing the problem of inadequate funds and wanting a larger federal focus on the western states, Bureau of Indian Affairs director John Collier decided to divide American Indian populations into three groups based upon his view of their level of acculturation. According to Laurence Hauptman, "among the tribes listed by Collier as acculturated peoples 'capable' of operating without the bureau were 'New York Indians.'"[5] Hauptman accurately summed up the ongoing situation between New York State and American Indians when he said that "while state politicians and reformers frequently referred to the so-called 'Indian problem' as being in dire need of a solution, the Indians have historically perceived Albany policy and policymakers as their main problem."[6] The various recognized nations of the Haudenosaunee have all faced and continue to face complications and challenges to their community identity and existence.

However, in terms of nonrecognized communities, the Mohawks have had ongoing conflicts with the state of New York over land and sovereignty relating to the Saint Regis reservation. The Ganienkeh "crisis" (at least a crisis for New York State) has been an issue since the Moss Lake occupation in 1974 and remains an unresolved issue for New York State and Clinton County.[7] In May 1974, a group of Mohawks from reservations in both Quebec and New York took over and occupied a 612-acre site near Moss Lake. The potential for violence and bad press for New York State moved then New York secretary of state Mario Cuomo to negotiate the movement of the Ganienkeh Mohawks to parcels of land in Clinton County, where a small Mohawk community remains today. In his recent newspaper article, writer James Odato says that "the Ganienkeh inhabitants consider the state property reclaimed Mohawk land and themselves a sovereign nation. They have kept out interlopers, especially anyone with illegal drugs or alcohol, with their own police force." Since receiving this land, they have used the trust that owns the land to acquire an additional 1,700 acres in tax-exempt property.[8]

This leads to some fundamental questions about what the political and legal status of the Ganienkeh Mohawks is and perhaps even their status should be. It seems that the actions of New York State in providing land to be held by a trust could indicate their treatment of the Ganienkeh Mohawks as a separate Mohawk entity; however, New York State Indian law does not include a section on this group, and the state does not recognize them as a governmental entity. Additionally, the federal government has not commented one way or the other. This issue is compounded by the fact that we are now forty years (and thus likely also a few generations) removed from the social context in the Mohawk reservation communities of Akwesasne and Kahnawake that produced the original 1974 takeover. In a news story in 2005, staff writer Suzanne Moore indicated that the position of the Ganienkeh residents remains that they are neither New York State nor U.S. citizens, but are instead citizens of their Mohawk Nation.[9] In 2006, Forty-Fifth District state senatorial candidate Tim Merrick indicated that he was in favor of "exploring the federal recognition process for this tribe, which could result in sovereign lands."[10] In a further complication, the Seneca Nation of Indians and the Saint Regis Mohawks withheld millions of dollars in payments to New York State in 2010. These payments are revenue generated from casinos operated under state gaming compacts. They indicated that they were withholding the money due to issues related to the larger New York State–American Indian relationship. One of the main issues is the existence of other gaming operations in New York State, which in their view makes the state in violation of those compacts.[11] Part of the controversy remains the relationship between Ganienkeh and Saint Regis and the (illegal) gaming operations run by the Ganienkeh Mohawks. The overall point here is that the Mohawks at Ganienkeh are clearly known to exist, but they are not formally acknowledged in a political or governmental sense by the state or federal governments. They are not recognized as a separate and independent nation (which they desire), nor are they recognized as a "domestic dependent nation."

In addition to the Ganienkeh community, the Kanatsiohareke Mohawk community was established in 1993 and is located near the Village of Fonda in Montgomery County. While established by a peaceful relocation of Mohawks from Saint Regis (and the adjacent Akwesasne Reserve in Canada), this community sits in a unique position on the historical Mohawk land base.[12] The Kanatsiohareke Mohawk also currently exist as an indigenous community without explicit state or federal recognition. The reestablishment of a Mohawk community in their traditional homeland in the Mohawk River Valley was neither a new idea, nor one without a history of conflict and incident. In 1958, Elmer Buckman of Fort Hunter retained attorney Charles S. Tracy to "seek a court order for the ejection of a band of Mohawk Indians who, he said, were camping on his property" since 1957. This case resulted in a court order by Judge Chandler S. Knight to vacate the property by April 1. The Mohawk leader Frank Johnson and his followers were threatened by the sheriff's office with forced removal and arrest if they refused. The leadership of the Iroquois Council at Onondaga had already moved many of the Mohawks to the Onondaga Reservation by the time the court order was enacted; however, Johnson and another Mohawk, Peter Beauvais, chose to remain. The incident became known as the "Invasion of June 1957," and the Mohawks along Schoharie Creek near Fort Hunter were deemed by the county court to have "no authority to be where they were." The huts built by the Mohawks were mysteriously burned "by persons whose connection with the court ordered evacuation remains unknown."[13]

The issue regarding the Kanatsiohareke Mohawks is not whether they have a right to be there, but is one of understanding their status as individuals and as a community either within or outside of the legal parameters of the state and federal governments. Their ambiguous community status constitutes a problem of legibility for those external governments. If these Mohawks are to be understood as citizens of the federally recognized Mohawk government at Saint Regis, then their status as federally recognized Indians could place specific issues before the state and federal officials, especially regarding treaty rights and the federal or state provision of services to Saint Regis Mohawks now residing at Kanatsiohareke. The position of the Saint Regis-Akwesasne community on the international border of the United States and Canada creates the potential for further complications, including the likely presence of Mohawks at Kanatsiohareke who are not U.S. citizens. While these two communities of Ganienkeh and Kanatsiohareke may not view the issue of external political and legal recognition as a "problem," they will surely continue to confound state and federal government officials in the years to come.

The politically recognized American Indian populations on Long Island consist of the (as of 2010) federally recognized Shinnecock Indian Nation and the state-recognized Unkechaug Nation. Partly because of the early recognition of their lands by the English Crown, these two acknowledged tribal nations still maintain established communities and reservations on Long Island that have remained relatively intact despite being surrounded by non-Indians since the late seventeenth century. In the 1915 report of the Department of the Interior, the Poospatuck (Unkechaug) and the Shinnecock Indians were listed in tables entitled "Indian Population of the United States," demonstrating that the federal government was aware of the existence of these two Indian communities.[14]

Historically, the relationship between the non-Indian residents of Long Island and the American Indian populations has not always been amiable: claims over the "Indian-ness" of the tribal nations, as well as their right to exist as reservation communities, have been challenged in the popular media and in court.[15] In 1936, local landowner William S. Dana wanted the state to declare that the Poospatuck Reservation (home to the Unkechaugs) was not an Indian reservation, which would allow him to claim title to the land and evict them. Dana launched a private action to evict the Unkechaugs as squatters, hiring former judge John R. Vunk to represent his interests. The Unkechaugs were successful in their legal opposition, because they were able to demonstrate their descent from the Unkechaug people named in the original land grant in 1700.[16]

In addition to these two recognized American Indian nations, there are other American Indian communities on Long Island, which further complicates the political and ethnic makeup of New York State. There are at least two documented American Indian populations still living on Long Island that are not recognized politically by either the state of New York or the federal government. These are the Montauketts (also known as the Montauks) and the Matinnecocks.

The Montauketts, both historically and today, live on the eastern end of the island near what is now East Hampton. In 1910, in the state court decision for *Wyandank v. Benson (1909)*, Judge Abel Blackmar ruled that the Montauketts no longer existed as a distinct tribal community. The Montauketts brought the lawsuit against local property owner Arthur Benson, claiming that the land transactions of 1885, 1893, and 1903, in which Benson acquired the remainder of Montaukett land holdings, were illegal and therefore invalid.[17] To put it in simple terms, the Montauketts were terminated by a New York State court decision in a case brought by them to regain their traditional homeland. While it is certainly more than reasonable to question whether a state court has the authority to proclaim a people administratively extinct, what is of particular note in this court decision was the rationale for denying the existence of the Montauketts. In the decision and in those of the subsequent appeals, the Montauketts were denied their existence on racial grounds. The courts said the Montauks had mixed with "inferior races" and that they were "impaired by racial miscegenation, particularly with the negro race."[18] In essence, the Montauks were terminated not because they could not prove their community existence or their Indian bloodline, culture, and identity, but rather because they had intermarried with local African Americans beginning in the eighteenth century. The judge used a version of what is known sociologically in the United States as the "one-drop rule" of hypodescent (in which a person is classified as "black" even if they possess only a small amount of African ancestry) to deny the existence of an entire indigenous people.

Though this rationale was used for their case, mixed racial ancestry is common in the indigenous communities on Long Island, as well as throughout coastal New England.[19] In fact, all of the four existing American Indian communities on Long Island have a mixed racial history.[20] Due to the loss of land and economic independence, by the eighteenth century, it was common for indigenous peoples (both men and women) to work as either free laborers or indentured servants on the estates of local English landowners. Additionally, in the eighteenth and early nineteenth centuries, American Indian men were often recruited to work on ships in the New England whaling industry, for which Sag Harbor, Long Island, was a prominent port.[21] Both of these situations placed these American Indians into prolonged contact with blacks and whites of similar socioeconomic status in the region who labored alongside them as slaves, indentured servants, and wage laborers. However, while acknowledging this mixed racial history, the indigenous populations of Long Island have continued to view themselves as American Indian communities.[22] Additionally, as historian John Strong documents in his 2001 book *The Montaukett Indians of Eastern Long Island*, the Montaukett people continue to exist as a people into the twenty-first century despite their official termination over a century ago.[23]

In contrast to the other Long Island groups, considerably less has been written about the Matinnecocks. The modern Matinnecock community is discussed somewhat by Strong, but the most in-depth scholarly examination of the modern Matinnecock community is William Hawk's 1984 doctoral dissertation, "The Revitalization of the Matinnecock Indian Tribe of New York." Historically, the Matinnecocks lived on the north shore on the western side of Long Island primarily in what is now Nassau County. According to Hawk, in the twentieth century the largest clusters of Matinnecocks lived in the areas of Flushing-Great Neck and Smithtown on the north shore of the island, and Swan Creek and Amityville on the south shore. Hawk states that cultural revitalization efforts had been underway in these communities since the 1950s. Unlike the Montauks, the Matinnecocks did not experience a singular moment in which they lost their official recognition as indigenous. Their proximity to New York City resulted in the Matinnecocks losing their lands and being erased from most of the historical record by the late seventeenth century. However, as Hawk demonstrates, they were able to persist as a loosely organized and landless population in their own homelands through the twentieth century.[24]

Hawk includes in his dissertation a brief section on the relationship between the New York Iroquois and the Matinnecocks during the process of Matinnecock cultural revitalization. It is illuminating and worth including here because it demonstrates both the racial tensions between indigenous peoples and the powerful symbolic role that Iroquois people have in understandings and representations of New York/northeastern indigeneity. On the racial issue, writing in 1984, Hawk states that there was hostility between the Matinnecocks and Iroquois people living in the New York City area. On top of the historical animosity between the Iroquois and the Algonquian peoples of New England and southern New York, derived from numerous wars during the colonial period in the seventeenth century, lie social and racial tensions around the idea of indigenous identity and authenticity. Hawk states that the Matinnecocks are generally dismissed by the Iroquois; according to Hawk's Matinnecock informants, some Iroquois in New York City are even "openly contemptuous of 'niggers dressed up in feathers'" at the pan-Indian powwows. Hawks adds:

> Matinnecocks resent the Iroquois, and they have reason
> to. Both groups have intermarried with non-Indians extensively, but Matinnecock racial identity was thereby compromised. That of the Iroquois was not. When Whites in
> New York talk about New York Indians, they mean upstate
> Iroquois, not Long Island Algonkians. The popular image
> of the Iroquois is formidable, their Indianness beyond
> question. That of the Matinnecocks is vulnerable and
> constantly impugned.

The racial issue can be clearly seen here as the relationship between racial mixture and authenticity. In the racialized construction of indigenous identity, Iroquois authenticity partly persists because their racial mixture occurred largely with whites; for groups like the Matinnecock, their racial mixture with blacks is more phenotypically apparent and viewed as representing their supposed tribal disintegration. Additionally, while Hawk states clearly that the New York Iroquois have "played no direct role in the Matinnecock revival," the Iroquois have had an indirect influence on the course of Matinnecock revitalization. Hawk explains that the "Matinnecocks may not like the Iroquois, but they have borrowed Iroquois traits with no hesitation." The Matinnecocks have adopted the common English translations for Iroquois cultural institutions such as longhouse, clan mother, and faith-keeper because of their popularity and commonly accepted authenticity as labels among both indigenous and non-indigenous audiences. This was done with the thinking that "authentic labels, even those of enemies, can serve as building blocks of native identity."[25]

OTHER HISTORICALLY KNOWN AND NONRECOGNIZED AMERICAN INDIAN PEOPLES IN NEW YORK

In addition to the Iroquois communities and the Long Island indigenous communities, there are also a number of known indigenous and "mixed" communities that have inhabited various regions of New York State in the twentieth century and have been identified in the academic literature, especially in that of anthropology. Some of these groups have a known tribal identity, while others were simply identified by scholars as belonging to a biracial or triracial isolate community where American Indian was one of these component races.[26] For example, in the 1948 annual report of the Smithsonian Institution there was a section entitled "Surviving Indian Groups of the Eastern United States." For New York, the author William H. Gilbert discusses the six nations of the Iroquois; the remaining tribes on Long Island (Shinnecock, Poosepatuck, Montauk, Setauket, and Matinnecock); a community of Abenakis at Lake George; and the smaller Indian groups along the Hudson River, Schoharie Valley, and elsewhere.[27]

An interesting note is that records show that Abenaki students from Lake George, New York, were among those sent to the federally administered Carlisle Indian Industrial School. This clearly demonstrates that the federal government was aware of the Abenaki community in Lake George and felt a need to utilize the boarding school in order to "civilize" them, indicating by default that they were not sufficiently "Americanized." The fact that some Abenakis who attended Carlisle lived in Lake George, New York, was even used by the state of Vermont in an attempt to refute the Vermont-based Saint Francis/Sokoki Band of the Abenaki Nation's petition for federal recognition.[28] Thus, on the one hand the governments recognized these children as sufficiently American Indian to send them to a government-funded boarding school for American Indian children, but contradictorily neither the U.S. government or the state of New York consider the community sufficiently American Indian for political recognition.

Gilbert identifies the Hudson River Indian groups as the "Bushwackers" (also known as "Pondshiners") living in Columbia County and in another grouping west of Newburgh. An American Indian isolate group living in the hills north of Albany in Rensselaer County was called the "Van Guilders." Additionally, the "isolate" groups of the Schoharie Valley include the "Slaughters," the "Honies," and the "Clappers." The "Nams," a group first reported in 1912, and the "Jukes," a group first described in the nineteenth century, are also reported as living in upstate New York.[29] Additionally, a group called the "Yanses" settled in the Albany Hill area of Schenectady in the beginning of the nineteenth century.[30] Finally, the rather extensive "Jackson Whites," living in Orange and Rockland Counties, constituted a distinct community of approximately 5,000 people in Gilbert's time.[31]

Calvin Beale reported on what he called "American Triracial Isolates" in 1957 and "mixed racial isolates in the United States" in 1972, meaning communities of people who possess European, African, and American Indian ancestry.[32] To this regard, Beale states that the American Indians listed on the 1950 U.S. census "do not constitute the sole biological legacy of the aboriginal population once found in the east."[33] Beale briefly describes the "Bushwackers" of Columbia County and the "Jackson Whites" of Orange and Rockland Counties in New York. In 1972, a decade and a half after his original research, Beale concluded that the "existence of mixed racial [American Indian] populations . . . constitute a distinctive segment of society."[34] In his book on the subject, *Almost White,* Brewton Berry mentions several of these New York groups including the Jukes, the Van Guilders, the Bushwackers, the Honies, the Clappers, the Slaughters, and the Jackson Whites. Additionally, William S. Pollitzer mentions some of these groups, specifically the Bushwackers and Jackson Whites, as residing in the lower and mid-Hudson valley. Likewise, in his 1953 article entitled "A Geographic Analysis of White-Negro-Indian Racial Mixtures in Eastern United States," Edward T. Price identifies the groups in New York known as the Slaughters, the Bushwackers, and the Jackson Whites.[35] There are, therefore, multiple instances throughout the nineteenth and twentieth centuries when scholars have reported the existence of American Indian communities or "mixed-race" communities with an identifiable American Indian component living in New York.

It is perhaps useful to note that many of the names used to describe these "isolate" peoples were developed by outsiders and were either derogatory labels or based on popular legend about the origins of the particular group. The so-called Jackson Whites are a classic example of this, and Daniel Collins and David Cohen both discuss the origin of the Jackson Whites label for that American Indian mixed-racial community living in the Ramapo Mountains in the border region of New York and New Jersey.[36] While New York does not recognize any of these groups as either American Indian peoples or political communities, in contrast, the state of New Jersey does formally recognize similar populations including, since the early 1980s, the group now known as the Ramapough Lenape Nation (formerly Jackson Whites). As a side note, it is possible that the absence of any federally recognized tribes in New Jersey could contribute to some of this difference in policy between New York and New Jersey. However, this explanation is flimsy because it does not explain why Vermont, which also lacks any federally recognized tribes, would deny the existence of Abenaki people in that state and resist their efforts at attaining formal recognition from the state and federal governments.

DISCUSSION

After this review, it is likely that a reader would have many questions. Why are some communities recognized while others are not? What has contributed to notions of "legitimate" versus "illegitimate" indigeneity? And what is the role of outside institutions in shaping and framing these discourses of legitimacy? For the purposes of comparison, Les Field's work with unacknowledged or nonrecognized tribes in California is useful for beginning to address these points.[37] Though the colonial histories of New York and California are certainly different and the justifications for nonrecognition in these two locations are also somewhat different, the important theme that can be drawn from Field's work that is relevant to New York and the East in general is the work of scholars in the legitimization process. Speaking specifically of anthropology, though the same is likely true to an extent for the other social sciences, Field says that "anthropological knowledge productions about indigenous peoples (in particular) has been historically linked to the bureaucratic systems nation-states developed and deployed in order to at least control and sometimes destroy indigenous cultures and societies."[38] Field continues by saying that

> anthropology's power with respect to native peoples of the United States should be understood as a series of relationships between, on the one hand, the "official anthropology" elaborated and promoted by the government bureaucracies charged with developing U.S. policies toward native peoples, and, on the other hand, the work of academic anthropologists in universities. Official anthropology is an outcome of the ways that the U.S. nation-state has used classificatory and categorizing schemes derived from academic anthropology as well as other sources to demarcate native identities.[39]

One of the key points to understand here is that although it may not be scholars' intention, the way that they frame and discuss different indigenous populations can contribute (and often has contributed) to the bureaucratic legitimization and political recognition of those populations, as well as of course the delegitimization and nonrecognition of other populations. The problem might not be the social scientists in academia specifically, since they are usually not the ones making those bureaucratic decisions about recognition. However, what they say about indigenous peoples, particularly the manner in which they discuss them and the terms used to describe them, do find their way into the thinking of policymakers and the decisions of the bureaucrats charged with implementing those policies. As such, anthropologists have often, either knowingly or unknowingly, given the backing of scientific authority to colonial and assimilationist policies. Field notes that this is why as an anthropologist his work consciously supports the acknowledgment and recognition of California's nonrecognized tribes.[40]

One major example of how this discourse and labeling can shape how scholars, government officials, and even the general populace understands and views a community in the East is the very notion of mixed-racial or triracial isolates. In some sense, the term is somewhat descriptively accurate since the communities for which it is used do have a mixed racial history. However, the term has a few major problems, all of which relate to the politicized context in which the term was developed and in which it was used. For one, the term is external in origin, meaning that it was not developed by those indigenous communities to describe themselves; rather, it was developed by scholars in the early twentieth century to describe what they perceived as social and biological anomalies of racial admixture.

Secondly, the term detribalizes, de-ethnicizes, and de-historicizes the community by framing them and discussing them simply in racial terms. While some American Indian ancestry is obviously acknowledged in order for them to be classified as "triracial," the mixed-racial label and the racial description implies that a tribal identity or ethnicity is either not known or that it is irrelevant, and that their occurrence is seemingly random instead of being a production of the complex social history of the region. Scholars' failure to specify tribal or ethnic identity and history portrays these people as not being legitimately indigenous, and instead implies that they are some type of exotic and illegitimate other. In that sense, the description of someone or some community as a triracial isolate can be understood as a process of "othering" and delegitimizing on the part of the scholar who possesses that authority and power of discourse and labeling. It may be true that in some of these detribalized indigenous communities there might be very little information and knowledge internally on the tribal origins of the community; however, the process of delegitimization by othering has been used against populations with a known ethnic and tribal identity and history (i.e., the Long Island tribes) as well.

It would be difficult to overstate the importance of race (and specifically blackness) in understanding this process of delegitimization by othering. As was said, many of these communities have known black/African ancestry, and in the minds of scholars and government officials of the time (and perhaps still now), racial "impurity" (especially black heritage) did not mesh with their ideas about what was an authentic and legitimate Indian. To this general idea, Eva Garroutte states that "although people must show only the slightest trace of 'black blood' to be *forced* (with or without their consent) into the category of 'African American,' modern American Indians must *formally* produce *strong* evidence of often rather *substantial* amounts of 'Indian blood' to be *allowed* entry into the corresponding racial category" (emphasis in original).[41] Additionally, many other indigenous populations in the East are known to be racially mixed both in the past and the present such as the Cherokee from the southern Appalachians region and even the Iroquois in New York, though they were not called mixed racial communities or mixed racial isolates. Thus a third problem with the term is that it was used primarily to describe populations with black/African ancestry, especially smaller communities. White ancestry was viewed externally as less polluting of authentic and legitimate indigeneity; and as anthropologists like Circe Sturm have demonstrated, these racial views against blackness have become internalized and reproduced by indigenous people over time.[42] While race was a common reason for refusing to recognize indigenous communities, there were other reasons. The small population size of many of these communities (hence the "isolate" label) has meant that they have been easy for the state to ignore and forget. Bonita Lawrence states that "some tribes . . . are not federally recognized because they were never at war with the United States and did not sign any treaties" and that "many of the tribal groups in the eastern United States . . . have avoided contact with the government . . . but have retained their identity; occasionally such groups are recognized by state governments but not by the federal government."[43] Similarly, their presence in the parts of the state that were colonized early meant that their histories and often times even their ethnic identities were suppressed and erased long before scholars took an interest in them. Likewise, once a colonizer has usurped ownership and dominion over land there is no purpose in continuing to make treaties with an indigenous community, and thus by default the community loses any formal acknowledgment of their existence that they may have once had, as was clearly the case for the Matinnecocks.

In studies that engage the topic of American Indians, especially the identity of people or communities as American Indians, there are layers of political, social, cultural, and emotional baggage that one must first recognize as clouding the facts. In America, the colonizer has rewritten the history of the events and developed a cultural mythology over two hundred years in which he has convinced himself that colonization and the resulting treatment of the indigenous population was justified or perhaps even predestined. As Anne-Marie D'Hauteserre said, "Colonial histories were constructed to legitimize colonial conquests and to obfuscate Native representations, and they continue to obstruct the claims and civil rights" of indigenous people.[44]

A complicating factor in understanding indigeneity, historically and contemporarily, in the United States is the connection between identity, recognition, and community. As Hilary Weaver states, "there is little agreement on precisely what constitutes indigenous identity, how to measure it, and who truly has it," and "identity is shaped, in part, by recognition, absence of recognition, or misrecognition by others." Weaver adds that "identity is a combination of self-identification and the perceptions of others" and that "indigenous identity is connected to a sense of peoplehood inseparably linked to sacred traditions, traditional homelands, and a shared history as indigenous people."[45] This idea that "indigenous" does not simply describe an individual but also that individual's connection to and sense of belonging with a history, a community, and a geographic territory is crucial for understanding both internal indigenous definitions of self and peoplehood as well as definitions created by the colonizer. Internal and external validation are expressed in colonial relations of power through the official political recognition by the colonizer of indigenous communities as a whole. Thus through the relations of power inherent in the recognition process, the colonial government has made itself the arbiter of indigeneity and legitimacy for entire populations, and the colonizer expresses this legitimacy of indigeneity in the biased terms and standards of what Field called "official anthropology." The history of colonial relations and the power of discourse have even led many indigenous people to believe in, internalize, and support these colonial structures of recognition and legitimization as proper and correct. Weaver adds that "through internalized oppression/colonization, we have become our own worst enemy."[46]

In regards to the racial dimension, Weaver states that "some indigenous communities . . . have experienced significant racial mixing," which leads to the question of whether these "indigenous communities absorb outsiders, or were they absorbed into the American melting pot?"[47] The politicized relationship between and conflation of race and recognition is common and persistent in the East, but that is especially true in New York and the greater New England region where it frequently involves a history of racial mixture with blacks.[48] As can be seen easily in the histories of the Unkechaug and the Montaukett, the answer to Weaver's question is not merely intellectual speculation, but can have significant political and material consequences. Also, the answer to that question is often not made by that indigenous community internally, but instead is made by outsiders, and often through a colonial legal system or bureaucracy.

While this general question was answered favorably by the court for the Unkechaugs, the Montauketts were not as fortunate. It is also worth adding that although the Unkechaugs won their legal case, they and the Shinnecocks were still denied the option of organizing under the Indian Reorganization Act of 1934 (which would have involved federal recognition), in part because of their racial mixture. In January 1936, John Collier sent Allan Harper to visit with the Unkechaugs and the Shinnecocks to determine whether these groups would be included under the IRA. Harper spent a grand total of two days with these Long Island communities: one day at each reservation. On his visit to the Poospatuck reservation, Harper met with several white residents who opposed Unkechaug recognition, though Harper also visited the New York State–sponsored Indian school at Poospatuck. In his report, Harper ignored the recent court victory by the Unkechaugs and instead recommended against including the Unkechaugs and the Shinnecocks in the IRA process. Much of Harper's rationale was racially based, as he said that the Unkechaugs had been "submerged by the Negro"; of the children at the Indian school at Poospatuck, Harper said that there was "not one straight hair in the bunch."[49]

Another aspect of the relationship between American Indian tribal nations and the state is the almost constant refrain from many segments of U.S. society (including many scholars in the past) that the American Indian is becoming "extinct." The vanishing Indian, like a political talking point of the present day, has been repeated so many times throughout American history that after a while, hearing nothing else, people tend to not only believe it, but proclaim that it has already happened and then act accordingly. For example, a prominent figure in early American anthropology, Lewis Henry Morgan, wrote in his well-known 1851 book entitled *The League of the Ho-de-no-sau-nee or Iroquois* that

> The Iroquois will soon be lost as a people, in that night
> of impenetrable darkness in which so many Indian races
> have been enshrouded. Already their country has been
> appropriated, their forests cleared, and their trails obliter-
> ated. The residue of this proud and gifted race, who still
> linger around their native seats, are destined to fade away,
> until they become eradicated as an Indian stock. We shall
> ere long look backward to the Iroquois, as a race blotted
> from existence; but to remember them as a people whose
> sachems had no cities, whose religion had no temples, and
> whose government had no record.[50]

If this degree of inevitability was used to describe one of the most populous and powerful indigenous groups on the continent, then what of the smaller, regional or local communities; the surviving remnant bands; or the family-based clans who managed to exist outside of the purview of the state or national governments? If even the Iroquois were described in terms of the inevitably "vanishing Indian," it should then be easier to understand how smaller indigenous communities and "mixed-race" indigenous communities in New York (and throughout the East) could be either dismissed or forgotten completely in mainstream colonial discourse, and relegated to lesser status even in scholarly discourse.

Additionally, while identity and recognition are complicated issues in themselves, measuring a person's identity and measuring the indigenous community are especially complicated, particularly when this measurement is conducted by an outside agency (both governmental and nongovernmental). In the workings of a bureaucracy, Indian identity can be arbitrarily established, leading to undercounting and misclassification. The misclassification of indigenous and mixed-race individuals is quite common in bureaucracies across the country; however, for New York specifically, Richard Rose was able to demonstrate in his 2012 doctoral dissertation that there is a statistically significant discrepancy in numbers of American Indians between federal and state data sets for the majority of school districts in the state of New York.[51] Another notorious place of miscounting and misclassifying American Indians has been that of the U.S. census, especially where that has involved American Indians of mixed ancestry and the use of enumerators.[52]

Collectively, this means that even those people whom the United States government has already identified as American Indian are many times not considered or recorded as American Indian by those very agencies, and the same is true of state and local government agencies. If these types of institutional problems exist even for the classification and counting of federally recognized American Indians, what then of the indigenous people for whom the federal and state governments have not or have only intermittently called American Indian? They seem to have a very slim chance of being identified or recorded as American Indian, and thus run the risk of being completely left out of discussions not only about indigenous rights, but even about the existence of indigenous people in an area. Thus it is important to understand that undercounting and misclassification of indigenous people are not simply bureaucratic problems, but instead serve the functional purpose of erasing the documentable existence of indigenous peoples.

All of these points could be viewed as of even greater importance now due to developments in international law and standards about the treatment of indigenous people. Under the United Nations Declaration

on the Rights of Indigenous Peoples, passed by the United Nations
General Assembly on September 13, 2007, indigenous people

> have the right to self-determination . . . have the right to
> autonomy or self-government in matters relating to their
> internal and local affairs . . . have the right to maintain and
> strengthen their distinct political, legal, economic, social
> and cultural institutions . . . have the right not to be sub-
> jected to forced assimilation . . . have the right to manifest,
> practice, develop and teach their spiritual and religious
> traditions . . . have the right to revitalize, use, develop and
> transmit to future generations their histories, languages,
> oral traditions, philosophies, writing systems and litera-
> tures . . . [and the] right to participate in decision-making
> in matters which would affect their rights.[53]

In essence, for the first time in international law, indigenous people
have a right to exist as indigenous people. The UN declaration is not
limited to only politically recognized indigenous people or those who
reside on reservations, but includes all indigenous people. Thus the
groups discussed here might all have a potential stake in asserting their
rights and status as indigenous people regardless of the current political status (or lack thereof).

The declaration speaks to the issue of politically nonrecognized
American Indian populations when it says that UN member states have
specific obligations. If the bold statements in the declaration—such as
"states shall provide effective mechanisms for prevention of, and re-
dress for . . . any form of forced assimilation or integration"—are to
have substantive meaning, then they must be applied to those indigenous populations that have already been terminated, deemed to have
been assimilated, or otherwise denied recognition. The declaration
also specifically prohibits the member states from "any action which
has the aim or effect of depriving them [indigenous people] of their
integrity as distinct peoples, or of their cultural values or ethnic identities."[54] This puts community revitalization efforts by the Montaukett,
the Matinnecock, and the Mohawks in Ganienkeh and Kanatsiohareke,
as well as the Abenaki and Ramapough, into an international arena.

While it remains to be seen whether the official change of position by the Obama administration in the United States in favor of the
declaration will result in any substantive or meaningful changes for
indigenous peoples in the United States, the declaration itself remains in-
triguing for the questions and possibilities that it can open up for scholars, policymakers, and indigenous people themselves. The point here is
not to fetishize recognition or to promote a recognition-only approach
to indigenous politics and community development.[55] Rather, the point

is how the critical understanding and reworking of the very idea of recognition and who is doing (and who has done) the recognizing can be useful in advancing the political goals of indigenous people. This would also aid in removing the barriers between and the flawed dichotomies of real/fake and recognized/unrecognized indigenous groups, and possibly contribute to building greater solidarity and mutual recognition between indigenous communities. The declaration provides scholars with a different context in which to examine and critique recognition, and is one that can facilitate and promote thought beyond the limitations of the policies of the U.S. government. For instance, when scholars critique colonial notions of indigeneity and colonial systems of recognizing and legitimizing (as well as failing to recognize or delegitimizing) indigeneity, this potentially opens up intellectual space for reexamining these other populations who have existed and persisted outside of the existing rules for recognition. This allows us to think about some of these populations not simply in the narrow terms of the past—as forgotten remnant populations or anomalous oddities of racial admixture—but instead rethink and reevaluate them as indigenous communities and even in terms of their potential voice for self-determination. In short, not limiting ourselves to the examination of recognized reservation-based indigenous communities allows for the further expansion of postcolonial discourse in anthropology and the other social sciences, and should allow us to critically reexamine what actually constitutes an indigenous person and an indigenous nation in the twenty-first century.

AUTHOR BIOGRAPHIES

Samuel W. Rose is a PhD student in the Department of Anthropology at the State University of New York at Buffalo.

Richard A. Rose, EdD, is an adjunct faculty member in history and criminal justice at the Schenectady County Community College.

NOTES

1 James W. Oberly, *A Nation of Statesmen: The Political Culture of the Stockbridge-Munsee Mohicans, 1815–1972* (Norman: University of Oklahoma Press, 2005).

2 Laurence M. Hauptman, *Conspiracy of Interests: Iroquois Dispossession and the Rise of New York State* (Syracuse, N.Y.: Syracuse University Press, 1999); Laurence M. Hauptman, *The Iroquois Struggle for Survival: World War II to Red Power* (Syracuse, N.Y.: Syracuse University Press, 1986).

3 Laurence M. Hauptman, *Formulating American Indian Policy in New York State, 1970–1986* (Albany: State University of New York Press, 1988), 45.

4 New York State Assembly, *Report of Special Committee to Investigate the*

Indian Problem of the State of New York (Albany, N.Y.: The Troy Press Company, 1889).

5   Hauptman, *Formulating American Indian Policy*, 11.

6   Ibid., 3.

7   For information on the Ganienkeh crisis, see: Gail H. Landsman, *Sovereignty and Symbol: Indian–White Conflict at Ganienkeh* (Albuquerque: University of New Mexico Press, 1988); Gail H. Landsman, "Indian Activism and the Press: Coverage of the Conflict at Ganienkeh," *Anthropological Quarterly* 60, no. 3 (1987): 101–13; Gail Landsman, "Ganienkeh: Symbol and Politics in an Indian/White Conflict," *American Anthropologist* 87, no. 4 (1985): 826–39; Kwinn H. Doran, "Ganienkeh: Haudenosaunee Labor-Culture and Conflict Resolution," *American Indian Quarterly* 26, no. 1 (2002): 1–23.

8   James M. Odato, "Mario Cuomo's 1977 Casino Deal Creates Headache for Son, Unprecedented Lease Left Land Rights Issues Unresolved," *Albany Times Union,* May 14, 2012.

9   Suzanne Moore, "Ganienkeh Must Be Treated as a Sovereign, Spokesman Insists," *Press Republican News,* April 18, 2005.

10   "Senate Candidate Merrick Wants End to Untaxed Indian Sales," *North Country Gazette,* October 31, 2006.

11   Odato, "Mario Cuomo's 1977 Casino Deal."

12   "Our History," Kanatsiohareke Mohawk Community, http://www.mohawkcommunity.com/home/ourhistory.html.

13   "Knight Issues Written Order on Eviction of Mohawk Band," *Amsterdam Evening Recorder,* March 26, 1958, 6; Hauptman, *Iroquois Struggle for Survival,* 149.

14   United States Department of the Interior, Administrative Reports, Volume II, Indian Affairs Territories, 1915.

15   John A. Strong, *The Unkechaug Indians of Eastern Long Island: A History* (Norman: University of Oklahoma Press, 2011); Donald Treadwell, *My People, the Unkechaug: The Story of a Long Island Indian Tribe* (Amsterdam: Da Kiva, 1992).

16   Strong, *Unkechaug Indians,* 209–10.

17   John A. Strong, "Who Says the Montauk Tribe Is Extinct? Judge Abel Blackmar's Decision in *Wyandank v. Benson* (1909)," *American Indian Culture and Research Journal* 16, no. 1 (1992): 1–22; John A. Strong, "The Imposition of Colonial Jurisdiction over the Montauk Indians of Long Island," *Ethnohistory* 41, no. 4 (1994): 561–90.

18   Strong, "Who Says the Montauk Tribes Is Extinct," 11.

19   Tiffany M. McKinney, "Race and Federal Recognition in Native New England," in *Crossing Waters, Crossing Worlds: The African Diaspora in Indian Country,* eds. Tiya Miles and Sharon P. Holland (Durham, N.C.: Duke University Press, 2006), 57–79; Ann McMullen, "Blood and Culture: Negotiating Race in Twentieth-Century Native New England," in *Confounding the Color Line: The Indian–Black Experience in North America,* ed. James F. Brooks (Lincoln: University of Nebraska Press, 2002), 261–91.

20   Paul T. Lockman Jr. and William Hawk, "Black Native Americans on the East Coast: The Case of the Algonkian Remnants of Long Island," *Free Inquiry in Creative Sociology* 23, no. 1 (1995): 11–14; Ellice B. Gonzalez, "Tri-Racial Isolates in a Bi-Racial Society: Poospatuck Ambiguity and Conflict," in *Strategies for Survival: American Indians in the Eastern United States,* ed. Frank W. Porter III

(Westport, Conn.: Greenwood Press Inc., 1986), 113–37.

21 Strong, *Unkechaug Indians*; Russel Lawrence Barsh, "'Colored' Seamen in the New England Whaling Industry: An Afro-Indian Consortium," in *Confounding the Color Line*, 76–107.

22 John A. Strong, *We Are Still Here: The Algonquian Peoples of Long Island Today*, 2nd ed. (Interlaken, N.Y.: Empire State Books, 1998).

23 John A. Strong, *The Montaukett Indians of Eastern Long Island* (Syracuse, N.Y.: Syracuse University Press, 2001).

24 Strong, *We Are Still Here*; William Hawk, "The Revitalization of the Matinnecock Indian Tribe of New York" (PhD diss., University of Wisconsin–Madison, 1984).

25 Hawk, "Revitalization of the Matinnecock," 57–60.

26 Calvin L. Beale, "An Overview of the Phenomenon of Mixed Racial Isolates in the United States," *American Anthropologist* 74, no. 3 (1972): 704–10.

27 William Harlen Gilbert Jr., "Surviving Indian Groups of the Eastern United States," in *Annual Report of the Smithsonian Institution* (Washington, D.C.: Smithsonian Institution, 1948), 410–13.

28 William H. Sorrell (State of Vermont Attorney General), State of Vermont's Response to Petition for Federal Acknowledgement of the St. Francis/Sokoki Band of the Abenaki Nation of Vermont (Montpelier, Vt., 2003), 138, http://www.atg.state.vt.us/assets/files/RESPONSE%20to%20Abenaki%20Petition-Jan2003v.pdf.

29 Gilbert, "Surviving Indian Groups," 410–13.

30 N. Greene, *History of the Mohawk Valley: Gateway to the West 1614–1925*, *Vol.* 2 (Chicago: S. J. Clarke Publishing Company, 1925), 1165–74.

31 Gilbert, "Surviving Indian Groups," 410–13; William Harlen Gilbert Jr., "Memorandum Concerning the Characteristics of the Larger Mixed-Blood Racial Islands of the Eastern United States," *Social Forces* 24, no. 1 (1945): 438–47.

32 Calvin Beale, "American Triracial Isolates: Their Status and Pertinence to Genetic Research," *Eugenics Quarterly* 4, no. 4 (1957): 187; Beale, "Overview," 704.

33 Beale, "American Triracial Isolates," 194.

34 Beale, "Overview," 705.

35 Brewton Berry, *Almost White* (New York: The Macmillan Company, 1963), 23; William S. Pollitzer, "The Physical Anthropology and Genetics of Marginal People of the Southeastern United States," *American Anthropologist* 74, no. 3 (1972): 722; Edward T. Price, "A Geographic Analysis of White-Negro-Indian Racial Mixtures in Eastern United States," *Annals of the Association of American Geographers* 43, no. 2 (1953): 138–55.

36 Daniel Collins, "Racially-Mixed People of the Ramapos: Undoing the Jackson White Legends," *American Anthropologist* 74, no. 5 (1972): 107–27; David Steven Cohen, "The Origin of the 'Jackson Whites': History and Legend among the Ramapo Mountain People," *Journal of American Folklore* 85 (1972): 260–66; David Steven Cohen, *The Ramapo Mountain People* (New Brunswick, N.J.: Rutgers University Press, 1974).

37 Les W. Field, "Complicities and Collaborations: Anthropologists and the 'Unacknowledged Tribes' of California," *Current Anthropology* 40, no. 2 (1999): 193–210; Les W. Field, "Unacknowledged Tribes, Dangerous Knowledge:

The Muwekma Ohlone and How Indian Identities Are 'Known,'" *Wicazo Sa Review* 18, no. 2 (2003): 79–94.

38 Field, "Unacknowledged Tribes, Dangerous Knowledge," 79.

39 Ibid., 80.

40 Ibid., 91.

41 Eva Marie Garroutte, "The Racial Formation of American Indians: Negotiating Legitimate Identities within Tribal and Federal Law," *American Indian Quarterly* 25, no. 2 (2001): 231.

42 Circe Sturm, *Blood Politics: Race, Culture, and Identity in the Cherokee Nation of Oklahoma* (Berkeley: University of California Press, 2002).

43 Bonita Lawrence, "Gender, Race, and the Regulation of Native Identity in Canada and the United States: An Overview," *Hypatia* 18, no. 2 (2003): 18.

44 Anne-Marie D'Hauteserre, "Explaining Antagonism to the Owners of Foxwoods Casino Resort," *American Indian Culture and Research Journal* 34, no. 3 (2010): 109.

45 Hilary N. Weaver, "Indigenous Identity: What Is It, and Who Really Has It?," *American Indian Quarterly* 25, no. 2 (2001): 240, 243, 245.

46 Ibid., 252.

47 Ibid., 244.

48 McKinney, "Race and Federal Recognition in Native New England"; McMullen, "Blood and Culture."

49 Strong, *Unkechaug Indians*, 221–28.

50 Lewis Henry Morgan, *League of the Iroquois* (New York: Carol Publishing Group, 1993[1851]), 145–46.

51 Linda Burhansstipanov and Deligh E. Satter, "Office of Management and Budget Racial Categories and Implications for American Indians and Alaska Natives," *American Journal of Public Health* 90, no. 11 (2000): 1720–23; Dorothy A. Rhoades, "Racial Misclassification and Disparities in Cardiovascular Disease among American Indians and Alaska Natives," *Circulation: Journal of the American Heart Association* 111 (2005): 1250–56; Nicholas Peroff, "Indian Identity," *The Social Science Journal* 34, no. 4 (1997): 485–94; Richard A. Rose, "American Indian Race and Ethnicity Data: An Historical Analysis and Comparison of NCES Data for NYS School Districts" (EdD diss., Sage Graduate School, 2012).

52 Angela A. Gonzales, "Racial Legibility: The Federal Census and the (Trans)Formation of 'Black' and 'Indian' Identity, 1790–1920," in *Indivisible: African–Native American Lives in the Americas*, ed. Gabrielle Tayac (Washington, D.C.: Smithsonian Books, 2009), 57–67; Jack D. Forbes, "Undercounting Native Americans: The 1980 Census and the Manipulation of Racial Identity in the United States," *Wicazo Sa Review* 6, no. 1 (1990): 2–26.

53 United Nations Declaration on the Rights of Indigenous Peoples (2007), http://www.un.org/esa/socdev/unpfii/documents/DRIPS_en.pdf.

54 Ibid.

55 Glen S. Coulthard, "Subjects of Empire: Indigenous Peoples and the 'Politics of Recognition' in Canada," *Contemporary Political Theory* 6, no. 4 (2007): 437–60.

The Decolonized Quadruple Bottom Line
A Framework for Developing Indigenous Innovation

Fonda Walters and John Takamura

Sustainable community development through innovation and entrepreneurship requires vast amounts of knowledge and involves multiple perspectives and contexts. The terms entrepreneurship, innovation, and sustainability have grown to be remarkably broad in context and meaning. These terms appear to be continually changing. For many, entrepreneurship has seemed to only exist in the realm of "for-profit" business; however, over the last several years the term entrepreneurship has emerged to include other contexts, for example green entrepreneurship, social entrepreneurship, and sustainable entrepreneurship. This essay examines the potential for further development of entrepreneurship within an indigenous or American Indian framework. A tailored and decolonized model of entrepreneurship—one more culturally relevant for indigenous and American Indian people and nations—potentially provides a perspective that can lead to a more functioning, viable economy for these communities and nations. Furthermore, this new model of indigenous and American Indian entrepreneurship and innovation is grounded in acknowledging the past, but more importantly has the potential to create sustainable indigenous/tribal economies in the immediate future.

The concept of a single bottom line has long been replaced by the triple bottom line of People, Planet, and Profit. The phrase "triple bottom line"—first coined by John Elkington, founder of the British consultancy SustainAbility, in 1994—suggests that companies ought to consider the three Ps: profit, in terms of gain and loss; people, in terms of an organization's social responsibility; and planet, in terms of an organization's responsibility to the environment. Elkington contends that an organization must measure each bottom line in order to gain an understanding of the full cost in doing business.[1] What the "triple bottom line" does not incorporate is an acknowledgment of culture or spirituality as a primary role in developing a sustainably sound entrepreneurial model fueled on innovation.

Community development by and for indigenous peoples and their communities has expanded the requirements for success in expressing the need for a quadruple bottom line—a four-faceted theoretical framework that incorporates indigenous concepts and perspectives. It is proposed that through a quadruple bottom line, based on factors unique to the indigenous experience, a specific type of innovation here referred to as *Indigenous Innovation* can be achieved.

There are several complex challenges related to contextualizing a framework from an indigenous mindset. In the case of American Indian people and nations, part of the challenge resides in the political status American Indian people hold as a result of the tumultuous relationship with the federal government. In most instances worldwide, indigenous people may not hold a similar political status outside their ethnic, social, or cultural presence in that part of the world. What indigenous people and American Indians do hold in common, however, is a shared past of colonization that has driven the direction of these nations and people.

This essay is an attempt to create a model that "decolonizes" the Western view of economic development, innovation, and entrepreneurship and reenvisions a model in which culture is the wellspring of innovation and entrepreneurship and ultimately supports an indigenous/ American Indian sustainable economic future. As Linda Tuhiwai Smith explains,

> Decolonization, however does not mean and has not
> meant a total rejection of all theory or research or Western
> knowledge. Rather, it is about centering our concerns and
> worldviews and then coming to know and understand
> theory and research from our own perspectives and for
> our own purposes.[2]

The decolonized quadruple bottom line is a framework for innovative strategies toward community development and nation building. This framework is based on the combination of *Community*, *Spirituality*, *Sustainability*, and *Entrepreneurship*, factors unique to indigenous peoples, and is used for sustainable enterprise creation. The overlap or combinations of each of these four factors leads to a subset of *Cultural*, *Social*,

Economic, and *Environmental* factors, also very much focused on indigenous perspectives. The overlapping factors located at the epicenter of the quadruple bottom line result in the creation of *Indigenous Innovation,* which is vital to the development of sustainable indigenous entrepreneurial ventures. This essay will define each of the four main factors of the quadruple bottom line (depicted in Figure 1) as well as each of the subset factors created by combining the four bottom lines and will describe the term "indigenous innovation" through a Native American and indigenous peoples perspective and context.

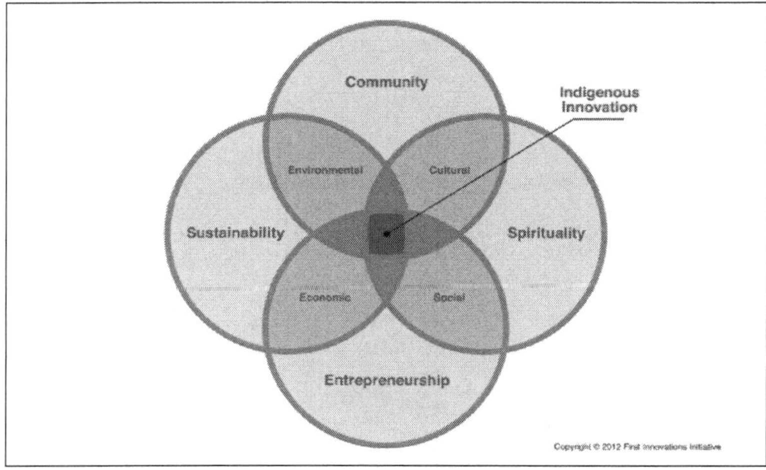

Figure 1. Quadruple bottom line, 2012. Courtesy First Innovations Initiative; copyright 2012.

The figure above depicts the four main factors and subsets of the quadruple bottom line that will be discussed throughout this essay.

COMMUNITY

The first of the factors in the decolonized quadruple bottom line is *Community.* "Community" is defined as any *indigenous* community, tribe, or group of people who have ties with a specific Native and or indigenous *cultural* identity. The defining of the term "indigenous" has proven to be difficult as it involves a multitude of evolving global sociocultural, sociopolitical, and socioeconomic contexts. In their essay, "Estimating the Number of Indigenous Peoples in Latin America," Layton and Patrinos describe the difficulties in defining the term "indigenous," given varying definitions between countries and scholarly reliance on language, self-identification by individuals, or research on indigenous concentrations within geographic territories.[3] Layton and Patrinos also refer to how social constructs of indigenous peoples are always evolving or changing and tend to be historical, cultural, and place-based and how indigenous indicators (dress, language, religion, and so on) are rarely fixed and or universal.[4]

In an attempt to address the social constructs of being indigenous in the context of global development, the World Bank Group's 2005 "Operational Policy 4.10" defines indigenous peoples as a distinct, often vulnerable, social and cultural group that not only self-identify as a member of such a group, but also have a specific attachment to geographic or ancestral territories. Distinct cultural norms or knowledge of economic, social, and political ways of knowing grounded in these territories and separate from dominant society, as well as established and unique foundations of language, further define indigenous peoples.[5]

The World Bank Group's 2003 "Operational Directive 4.20 on Indigenous Peoples" goes into more specific detail, adding terms to describe indigenous peoples such as "indigenous ethnic minorities, tribal groups or scheduled tribes" and stating that indigenous people are primarily subsistence-oriented in terms of wealth production.[6] The World Bank Group's definitions in both documents are purposely left broad in order to capture the diversity of peoples that fall under the category of "indigenous."

Creating an indigenous/American Indian framework for the purposes of decolonizing worldviews of entrepreneurship and innovation requires that "community" ultimately be defined through an indigenous/American Indian lens. It is in how these indigenous/American Indian communities or nations see themselves that the definition is found and where Indigenous Innovation can be created. The stark differences between communities and nations require an indigenous or tribally driven approach to defining the community or nation. Visioning who the community or nation is rests within the people themselves and is set in both ancestral knowledge of the past, as well as in present and future knowledge. Mindfully defining each factor (*Community, Spirituality, Sustainability,* and *Entrepreneurship*), separately and then in combination, leads to a framework of *Indigenous Innovation* that is strength based and created from an indigenous paradigm.

Cultural Contexts
[Community and Spirituality Factors Combined]

In even greater specification of "being indigenous" Corntassel sets forth a comprehensive definition of indigenous peoples based on the four interlocking concepts:

1. Peoples who believe they are ancestrally related, based on oral and/or written histories;

2. Peoples who tend to be community-based and reflect
   their distinct ceremonial cycles, kinship networks, and
   continuously evolving cultural traditions;
3. Peoples who speak (or once spoke) indigenous language,
   often with distinct dialects or uniquely indigenous
   expressions that may persist as a form of indigenous
   identity;
4. Peoples who distinguish themselves from the dominant
   society by residing in their traditional lands, which may
   be threatened by ongoing military, economic, or political encroachment, or by living in places to which they
   were expelled, while seeking to enhance their cultural,
   political, and economic autonomy.[7]

In contrast to the general definitions based on a global perspective like
that of the World Bank Group, here Corntassel's definition of indigenous peoples takes into account not only the historical but also the
ancestral aspects of indigenous peoples' homelands. He specifies both
formal as well as informal institutions that reflect the "continuously evolving cultural traditions" of indigenous communities. Although Corntassel
does not use the term "spirituality," he refers to the indigenous relationship with "ancestral homelands/sacred sites" and indigenous "ceremonial cycles" and "kinship networks."

Corntassel's reference to ancestral homelands and sacred sites
includes feeling connected to these places or activities (ancestral homelands and sacred sites, or ceremonies), regardless of whether an indigenous person has physically resided there or participated in such events.
Kinship networks in an indigenous mindset can exist in complex ways
in which being related to others through a clan system offers an extended network of family and community regardless of "blood" relationships. Community for indigenous/American Indian people may reach
far beyond physical boundaries and a general Western view of community. Concepts of family may also include significant clan and kinship
networks.

As Steckley asserts in his recent book on the clan-based system of
the eighteenth-century Wyandot, these clans served as critical and the
most important part of the society in areas of identity, strategic planning and problem solving, and determination of the political, economic,
and social structure.[8] Steckley's description of a clan system holds true
for example with the Navajo or Diné people. K'e is the Navajo term
that translates into English as compassion, cooperation, friendliness,
unselfishness, and peacefulness among other positive values that create an intense, diffuse, and enduring solidarity.[9] The Diné clan system
is derived from K'e and is the foundation for the connectedness and
relationship ties among the people. This matrilineal clan system creates

strong bonds and relationship to support a solidarity that is embedded in Diné values, traditions, cultural norms, and identity.

Indigenous worldviews of *Community* are essential in determining one of the four foundational elements to discovering and perpetuating *Indigenous Innovation* in order to pursue potential paths toward entrepreneurship and ultimately the sustainability of tribal nations.

SPIRITUALITY

The next factor in the decolonized quadruple bottom line is *Spirituality*. "Spirituality" encompasses indigenous *social* beliefs, values, and traditions. The idea of a quadruple bottom line that incorporates the concept of "spirituality" was first proposed by political scientist and futurist Sohail Inayatullah in his 2005 article, "Spirituality as the Fourth Bottom Line?" In that article Inayatullah defines spirituality as an inter-relationship of four factors:

(1) A relationship with the transcendent, generally seen as both immanent and transcendental. This relationship is focused on trust, surrender and for Sufis, submission.

(2) A practice, either regular meditation or some type of prayer (but not prayer where the goal is to ask for particular products or for the train to come quicker).

(3) A physical practice to transform or harmonize the body—yoga, tai chi, chi kung, and other similar practices.

(4) Social—a relationship with the community, global, or local, [and] a caring for others. This differs from a debate on whose God, or who is true and who is false, to an epistemology of depth and shallow with openness and inclusion toward others.[10]

Inayatullah's call for a fourth bottom line of spirituality is not intended merely as a reaction to modern societal progress. Inayatullah states that "for spirituality to become part of the global solution it will have to become transmodern, moving through modernity, not rejecting the science and technology revolution and the Enlightenment, nor acceding to postmodernity (where all values and perspectives are relativized) or the premodern (where feudal relations are supreme)." In essence, spirituality as the fourth bottom line must function as a means to bridge knowledge from the past to the present and from the scientific to other ways of knowing. The integration of "Spirituality" in a quadruple bottom line is unique to the indigenous experience in that it recognizes the value and importance of indigenous knowledge. Developers can learn much from locals who possess indigenous knowledge as they can act as expert informants. Ver Beek states that "the purpose of integrating 'indigenous' spirituality into development is neither to impose outside 'knowledge' nor to manipulate it as a means to the outsider's ends, but rather for mutual reflection and learning."[11]

Here Ver Beek points out the mutual benefits when outside experts and indigenous communities work together to integrate spirituality. Combining both indigenous knowledge and scientific knowledge will lead to more positive outcomes for both outside experts and indigenous communities. Ver Beek goes on to describe a three-step process for integrating spirituality; the first step begins with the outsider's efforts to gain knowledge of local (indigenous) knowledge through discussion, observation, and participatory research. The second step is to develop individual and community goals and to reflect on how local beliefs either aid or limit them. The final, third step involves making decisions about goals and how best to achieve them, accomplished as a community through blending outsider participation with indigenous knowledge and traditional values.[12] The integration of spirituality into a quadruple bottom line must ultimately involve a discussion based on mutual respect toward indigenous knowledge, traditions, and beliefs in order to foster successful community development.

As Smith explains, decolonizing theory and research doesn't necessarily mean a complete rejection of Western knowledge, rather it is a reassembly or reconstruction of theory and research from an indigenous mindset.[13] With the second element of *Spirituality* as a strategy incorporated into a decolonized framework of entrepreneurship and sustainability, *Indigenous Innovation* can become a vehicle in devising entrepreneurial business. Utilizing and acknowledging the indigenous spiritual connectedness to place, people, and values of community, this indigenously conceived framework thus can provide a stronger cultural match between business ventures and cultural integrity.

Indigenous Beliefs

Indigenous perspectives or worldviews are an important part of spirituality as they represent lasting indigenous beliefs carried through generations. To add to the strength-based understanding of *Spirituality* as a central element to a decolonized quadruple bottom line and the emergence of *Indigenous Innovation* as a framework for indigenous entrepreneurship, it is imperative to underscore the value of indigenous beliefs, knowledge, and values. Barnhardt and Kawagley affirm that although many indigenous peoples have gone through tumultuous social transformations, many have maintained their perspective or worldviews. They go on to state that "many of the core values, beliefs, and practices associated with those worldviews have survived and are beginning to be recognized as being just as valid for today's generations as they were for generations past."[14] Worldviews and indigenous beliefs, as Barnhardt and Kawagley contend, continue to be passed down to the next generations and to endure as viable and sustaining forms of knowledge systems.

Indigenous Knowledge

Indigenous knowledge differs from Western scientific knowledge and poses challenges in its adoption and integration on a global level. Morrison and Singh point out the differences between indigenous knowledge and scientific knowledge and state that "indigenous knowledge is interpreted in terms of belief systems, and contrasted to scientific knowledge systems held by the dominant global culture."[15] They go on to write, "This can be seen played out in how it is still highly problematic to consider that the quadruple bottom line includes spirituality as a reality rather than as merely a belief."[16] Morrison and Singh note that in order for spirituality to become the fourth bottom line, indigenous knowledge will need "open-mindedness" toward the sacred and divine belief systems of indigenous peoples. Only through the "authentic dialogue" between indigenous knowledge and scientific knowledge can spirituality truly be adapted within a quadruple bottom line.

Indigenous Values

Indigenous values have stemmed from a strong commitment to passing down sustainable traditional knowledge from the eldest to younger generations through many methods, but oral tradition is emphasized in many communities. Indigenous values generally acknowledge that it is the listener's responsibility to interpret the knowledge being transferred, which typically requires patience, time, and inner reflection from all parties. An indigenous worldview might also include acknowledging that life lessons may be derived from a number of varied sources, but striving toward "balance" is significant in all areas of one's life as well as recognizing and respecting the interconnectedness of human beings and their place in the world.[17]

Applying this context to a Western worldview of business and entrepreneurialism would prove to be challenging as "interconnectedness of human beings" is not a typical attribute of existing business thought, except for perhaps in emerging areas of green or social entrepreneurship. The discussion throughout this essay presents a compelling argument that indigenous peoples innately have an understanding of deep community, spirituality, and balance and that these values can spark or add strength to new models of indigenous innovation. The results are a decolonized entrepreneurship model that values indigenous knowledge, fosters the creation of indigenous entrepreneurship, and ultimately contributes to overall tribal sustainability.

Arizona State University Regents' Professor Simon Ortiz has explained "sustainability" from his perspective:

> Sustainability is the function and process of being fed,
> nourished, maintained, and provided for by the context
> within which one exists and lives. For people or the
> human community, it is a dependency upon the context
> within which they exist and live. And most importantly,
> it is the inter-dependent relationship that is central
> to the existence of both the human community and the
> context.[18]

He further contextualizes this definition of sustainability as informed through his personal Acoma Pueblo perspective, encapsulated by his traditional language and translated into English here: "We do not Exist for no purpose. We are not Alive for no reason. Always for the purpose and reason of helping the Land and the People, we are Existing-Living."[19] Wuttunee expands on this worldview:

> Truly understanding Indigenous values and perspectives
> requires a lifetime of commitment and dedication to an
> Indigenous worldview. Values are misunderstood because
> of a complexity that can only be studied and their true
> meanings identified in the original languages . . . Finally,
> while there are common values across Indigenous communities, any written recounting of those themes must be in
> a context that also acknowledges considerable diversity of
> practice and experience.[20]

Taking indigenous values and incorporating them into the larger concept of nation building can speak to their value in developing more effective sustainable tribal economic development. Connection to broader indigenously driven concepts of sustainability creates an opportunity to redefine what indigenous innovation and entrepreneurship can mean and how tribes may use this redefinition in building both tribal enterprise and tribal-citizen entrepreneurship.

Incorporating "cultural match" is mentioned as contributing significantly to nation building. Cornell and Kalt offer this list of central nation-building concepts:

- Practical sovereignty: practical decision-making power
  in the hands of Indian nations.
- Effective governing institutions: the effective patterns
  of organizations in which development has to take hold
  and flourish.

- Cultural match: when cultural match is high, economic development tends to be more successful.
- Strategic orientation: an approach to development that starts not with the question of "what can be funded?" but with "what kind of society are we trying to build?"
- Nation-building leadership: the primary concern is putting in place the institutional and strategic foundations for sustained development and enhanced community welfare.[21]

Cornell states that a gradual shift over the last twenty-five years, from transfer-based economies to productive ones, has transformed tribal nations.[22] He describes how for centuries Indian nations have been heavily dependent on transfer payments from the federal government, but during recent decades, productive economic activity is booming on Indian lands, although this change has been gradual and is not universal. In other words, economic activity might include both a limited or in some cases a non-transfer economy from the federal government and more self-determined economic activity within the tribal nations themselves.[23] Tribal gaming enterprises as well as other major ventures are examples of areas that are contributing toward more functioning tribal economies, but they are certainly not the silver bullet. Rather, they are perhaps only part of the puzzle that once completed will also share the economic space with others such as tribally owned, tribal-citizen entrepreneurship on all levels from small business to midsize and beyond. Respecting indigenous values is a critical component of a strong, decolonized model for business envisioned through indigenous eyes.

Social Contexts
[Spirituality and Entrepreneurship Factors Combined]

Decolonizing the western "triple-bottom line" by including spirituality is a dramatic shift from this long-recognized model of business. From an indigenous/American Indian framework and knowledge base, spirituality is always a critical component to a person/community/nation's well-being. In many indigenous cultures, spirituality is necessary to having balance within oneself and dealing with others and potentially is a path that can lead to productive decisions for continued sustaining of the community or nation as a whole. In developing a decolonized model of business, spirituality plays a crucial role in determining what projects and ventures are best suited to the individual/community/nation as it is an opportunity to gauge the projected outcomes against the vision the individual/community/nation has for itself.

The third factor within the decolonized quadruple bottom line is *Sustainability.* "Sustainability" refers to *economic* sustainability and re-silience as well as *environmental* sustainability, as covered in the following sections. Sustainability in the context of the essay is broader than the Western view of sustainability. Sustainability as Regents' Professor Ortiz stated is more encompassing, and for indigenous/tribal nations, sustainability is multifaceted, involving a functioning tribal economy, social ecological systems, and environmental contexts. Indigenous ways of knowing touch on all these areas, and indigenous communities have an opportunity to incorporate this framework into strategically created tribal entrepreneurship opportunities.

Tribal Economy

Dependency is the leading theory offered by many experts in economics, American Indian studies, and political science to explain the economic situations of modern-day Indians.[24]

Dependency theory when applied to tribal nations explains the underdevelopment of tribes as the transfer of resources from low or peripheral areas (tribes) to more economically developed areas (dominant culture/system/country). This dynamic stalls the development of peripheral areas.[25]

Theorists have identified other consequences that arise from dependency: (1) economic activities in the peripheral regions are essentially controlled from the outside; (2) peripheral regions lack economic diversity and choice; (3) they suffer distortions in economic, social, and political conditions; (4) their subsistence systems collapse; (5) they come to rely on the economic core areas; and (6) social vacuums result in the establishment of new dependent institutions and economic practices. Anyone familiar with Indian Country and its history, and federal Indian law and policies, will recognize many of these factors.[26]

Miller acknowledges that there are a few scholars who criticize dependency theory. He notes that Brian Hosmer has suggested that the dependency theory ignores the complexity of culture, assuming that underdeveloped, "backward" people will remain that way and failing to acknowledge how Indians have reacted to challenging situations.[27] Miller also mentions another critic of the dependency theory, Patricia Albers, who states that dependency theory operates at levels of abstraction where individual actors are hidden by the workings of larger systems. As a result, American Indians appear as pawns to forces and formations outside their control, and this denies American Indian people agency.[28] Lastly, Colleen O'Neill suggests that the dependency theory is "rife with internal tensions and contradictions" and that "universal assumptions about the relationship between capitalism and Native American culture . . . obscured the role of indigenous people in crafting alternative strategies or pathways of development."[29]

We suggest, similarly, that the same general criticisms can apply in regard to the lack of functional tribal economic development and specifically to the concepts of innovation, entrepreneurship, and American Indian sustainability. Much like trying to understand dependency theory and its application to indigenous/tribal affairs, understanding the lack of tribal economic development and tribal-citizen entrepreneurship is partially, if not wholly, related to viewing economic development and entrepreneurship solely from a Western worldview and not acknowledging the culture of indigenous/tribal people and nations.

Social Ecological Systems

Ostrom introduced a framework for the study of complex systems called the social-ecological systems (SES) framework.[30] SESs are complex systems often made up of several subsystems, resembling the multiple subsystems of organisms. Social-ecological system frameworks not only show the relationships between the multiple subsystems but also involve the related economic, political, and social settings. Ostrum describes these linked economic, political, and social settings in her overview of the subsystems in the SES framework through the example of a public park whose *resource systems* are comprised of a forested area, wildlife, and a water system. In the context of this park, *resource units* are the trees and plants, the varieties of wildlife, and amount and flow of water. The *governance systems* include the local governing body or organization that oversees the park and sets the rules. The *users (actors)* would be anyone who comes to the park for recreation, employment, and so on.[31] The interaction between resource systems, resource units, governance systems, and users (actors) leads to outcomes that are ultimately affected by the broader social, economic, and political context.

Indigenous/American Indian people can be seen as the "actors" in a social-ecological system (SES) who must face the social, economic, and political forces and formations within the system. Viewing indigenous communities as SESs will aid both developers as well as the communities themselves in overseeing the environmental impacts of activities and the long-term sustainability of the community. Furthermore, incorporating indigenous strongholds of community, spirituality, sustainability, and entrepreneurship can further inform and ultimately create indigenous innovation to solve challenges faced by tribal nations.

Environmental Contexts
[Sustainability and Community Factors Combined]

Chapin, Folke, and Kofinas, in their book *Principles of Ecosystem Stewardship,* describe the four main approaches or mechanisms to sustainability as *Vulnerability, Adaptive Capacity, Resilience,* and *Transformability.*[32] *Vulnerability,* based on socioeconomic studies, focuses on equity and well-being and is the "degree to which a system is likely to experience harm due to exposure to a specified hazard or stress."[33] *Vulnerability* as an approach to sustainability is concerned with the mitigation of stress on a system. It is related to the other sustainability approaches of *adaptive capacity* and *resilience* in that it aims to reduce stress by increasing *adaptive capacity* through experimentation and innovation, for example, and by increasing *resilience* through sustaining legacies that can lead to renewal.

Adaptive Capacity refers to the ability of actors to "respond to, create and shape variability" in a system.[34] This sustainability approach is primarily focused on human actors, and actions are based on past experiences incorporating biological, economic, and cultural diversity as well as reflexive action incorporating future planning, experimentation, and innovation. Adaptive capacity is the ability of a socioeconomic system to make social, human, natural, and built capital for "future generations to meet their own needs."[35] In short, adaptive capacity is a sustainability approach that seeks new states of a system through adapting to differential vulnerability stresses.

Resilience is "the capacity of a social-ecological system (SES) to absorb a spectrum of shocks or perturbations and to sustain and develop its fundamental function, structure, identity and feedbacks through either recovery or reorganization in a new context."[36] Resilience relates to adaptive capacity in that it also depends on past experiences (social memory) about how humans overcame past crises in addition to building the biophysical legacies that contribute to future states of the system. Resilience differs from conventional vulnerability in that it focuses on resource stewardship and management in the context of uncertainty (variability of stresses) in a wide range of spatial and temporal scales as opposed to only focusing on responses to known stresses.

Transformability focuses efforts on the reconceptualization of a system through paradigm shifts. Here a "fundamentally different set of critical slow variables, internal feedbacks, and societal goals" are developed in order to repair or improve the system. Resilience components, such as legacies, and adaptive capacity tools, such as biological, economic, and cultural diversity, help to enhance transformability by providing the "seeds" for new ideas; however, transformability often is the result of crises. These are what Chapin, Folke, and Kofinas refer to as "regime shifts" where transitions are abrupt and are the result of "persistent changes" in slow variables (for example, persistent grazing shifting grasslands into shrub lands).

Environmental contexts, specifically sustainable community contexts, must adopt a deep understanding of the sustainability approaches and mechanisms of ecosystem stewardship especially when entrepreneurial activities are a means toward building indigenous/American Indian communities. The decolonized quadruple bottom line framework focuses on the aforementioned environmental contexts in the overlapping areas of *Sustainability* and *Community* and plays a distinct role in encompassing broader views of how environmental contexts can inform strategic tribal nation-building efforts.

ENTREPRENEURSHIP

The fourth and final factor in the decolonized quadruple bottom line is *Entrepreneurship*. "Entrepreneurship" in this context is a redefinition of the term from the perspective of tribal economies and incorporates a unique blend of indigenous *social, economic,* and *socio-ecological* factors.

Economic Contexts
[Entrepreneurship and Sustainability Factors Combined]

Despite shared experiences of dramatic and extensive assaults upon indigenous and American Indian human rights, landholdings, culture, and sovereignty, indigenous people and nations have endured and persevered. Indigenous and American Indian peoples continually acknowledge this past that has driven them to protect and strengthen sovereignty, self-determination, and self-sufficiency for the future.

Historically, within the Americas, indigenous peoples had extensive knowledge of concepts such as property rights, principles of entrepreneurship, private business, and private property rights.[37] American Indian people have always been successful innovators and entrepreneurs, as the creators of major indigenous trade centers and networks, long before European contact. Agricultural food, garments, and a variety of other goods were traded not only among tribal nations, but between non-Native traders as well. Without indigenous innovation, we wouldn't be enjoying corn, chocolate, or items such as chewing gum or parkas. Indigenous innovation and entrepreneurial ventures that are high impact and high potential (for profit and nonprofit) potentially can be the basis for sustainable economies and vitality for indigenous nations and people.

In the era of prosperity for some American Indian tribes, particularly those who have been successful at gaming enterprises, one might wonder why the statistics for American Indians throughout the country are still startling. American Indian and Alaska Native populations living on reservations mostly are plagued by low educational attainment, high unemployment (more than twice the national percentage of all races combined), and significant rates of poverty.[38] It appears that tribal economic development and sustainability have additional complexities beyond developing tribal enterprises, small businesses, and limited citizen entrepreneurship, or even creating jobs. So how does one develop individuals who understand the complexities of tribal economic development and also can navigate and create their own innovative pathways?[39] Through decolonizing business, the quadruple bottom line model encompasses ideals already held in many indigenous communities or nations that can lead toward indigenous ways of driving and creating functioning, sustainable tribal economies.

Majid and Koe are among a handful of scholars who suggest a revised model of sustainable entrepreneurship that consist of four domains, namely economical, social, ecological, and cultural, which in their perspective should be given equal priority.[40] They provide examples of sustainable entrepreneurship that illustrate a variety of factors, but either disallow culture as a primary domain or emphasize one domain over another.

Miller and Collier call for a redefinition of entrepreneurship that borrows from leadership literature in that entrepreneurship could be viewed as taking two forms: 1) transactional entrepreneurship, and 2) transformational entrepreneurship.[41] Miller and Collier describe traditional entrepreneurship as a shift of economic resources from a lower to a higher area of productivity, while transactional entrepreneurship adds innovation as a central feature. Lastly, transformation entrepreneurship is described as a virtue-based, innovative organization whose focus is on shifting resources into areas of higher purpose and greater value, which ultimately requires a holistic perspective.[42]

Miller and Collier get closer to including culture as a part of entrepreneurship by incorporating this holistic perspective in their redefinition, which seems to align with indigenous ways of knowing, in which all things are connected.

Majid and Koe discuss other redefinitions of entrepreneurship that heavily involve sustainability, an emphasis on the environment, or value creation that contributes to sustainable development.[43] They point out that a cultural context should be included. Majid and Koe further contend that "balancing among the three aspects of social, environmental and economic remains as the main challenge for most businesses" and "reconciling these three domains in an equal manner remains difficult and challenging."

Perhaps indigenous innovation and entrepreneurship is already encompassed within indigenous values and therefore there is less "reconciliation" to be done within a theoretical model that supports the four domains of economic, social, environmental, and culture from the inception. Rather, the four domains as discussed in this essay are already embedded as indigenous knowledge and knowing that supports innovation and entrepreneurship when contextualized from an indigenous framework. In this vein, decolonizing the Western approach to innovation and entrepreneurship would innately acknowledge and embed culture as a significant element to an indigenous model of innovation and entrepreneurship.

Wuttunee, Loustel, and Overall further suggest that incorporating indigenous values bodes well for indigenous peoples and their businesses in three ways:

1. any corporate strategy that compels a more holistic focus on society will undoubtedly involve both indigenous peoples and their businesses;
2. as companies pursue a CSR (Corporate Social Responsibility) approach undoubtedly new business opportunities will arise that respect, embrace and utilize indigenous values and capacities;
3. given both its rich and diverse history of holistic, community thinking, indigenous leaders and businesses can offer mainstream businesses unique and valued perspectives that may increase understanding and success in implementing CSR.[44]

This essay strives to continue this optimistic view by starting to build a theoretical decolonized model of indigenous innovation and entrepreneurship that organically includes culture as a primary element regarding economic contexts of indigenous/American Indian peoples.

INDIGENOUS INNOVATION

Finally, the term "indigenous innovation" refers to the specific type of innovation that occurs within indigenous communities from the combination of *Community, Spirituality, Sustainability,* and *Entrepreneurship:* factors unique to indigenous peoples. *Indigenous Innovation* exists in the epicenter of the decolonized quadruple bottom line and can only be achieved through the holistic blending of all the aspects discussed in the previous four sections.

The systems thinking and the design thinking approaches are integral to understanding the general concept of innovation, leading toward a proposed decolonized model and forming the epicenter of indigenous innovation. They also further ground the existing literature that finally provides the conclusion of this essay with a diagram of the decolonized quadruple bottom line.

Systems Thinking

Within the context of innovation, the systems thinking approach is vital to developing a holistic point of view regarding community development and social entrepreneurship. Metcalfe and Ramlogan refer to the idea of "innovation systems" and state that "since systems require connections as well as components, it is the formation of the connections, which is the necessary step in the creation of any innovation system."[45] They go on to state that "innovation systems do not occur naturally, they self-organise to bring together new knowledge and the resources to exploit that knowledge; and the template they self-organise around is . . . the problem sequence that defines a particular innovation opportunity."[46] Metcalfe and Ramlogan point out that the systems of innovation are emergent phenomenon that will evolve based on the contexts that surround their development. Stepler, Garguilo, Mehta, and Bilen introduce the notion of "systems thinking" and state that "systems thinking encourages a holistic view of development challenges" and that "areas targeted for intervention are looked at as part of a complex web of interconnected and interacting systems and subsystems."[47] The authors further explain that this holistic view "forces attention on the larger picture and wider processes of change rather than concentrating on discrete outputs at the project level." They contend that such a holistic view can counter issues or subsystems that may be overlooked or unforeseen. In this sense, systems need to be "designed" to meet not only the goals of the subsystems but also the goals of the entire system.

Design Thinking and Innovation

Brown and Wyatt describe design thinking as made up of the three distinct components of *Inspiration, Ideation,* and *Implementation.*[48] In their explanation, they recommend thinking of "*inspiration* as the problem or opportunity that motivates the search for solutions; *ideation* as the process of generating, developing, and testing ideas; and *implementation* as the path that leads from the project stage into people's lives." They go on to say that design thinking is not necessarily a lockstep iterative process and that it may loop back on itself through the inspiration, ideation, and implementation phases.[49]

The term "design" is often used in the context of innovation both as a noun and as a verb in that design is both a process and a system. Brown states that "the design process is best described metaphorically as a system of spaces rather than a predefined series of orderly steps." Brown goes on to assert that this system of spaces "demarcate different sorts of related activities that together form the continuum of innovation."[50]

Although design has long been associated with companies and the innovation around their products and services, design is also an important part of social innovation. Brown and Wyatt in their article *Design Thinking for Social Innovation* state that "businesses are embracing design thinking because it helps them be more innovative, better differentiate their brands, and bring their products and services to market faster." The key points that Brown and Wyatt make are that:

> Nonprofits are beginning to use design thinking as well to develop better solutions to social problems. Design thinking crosses the traditional boundaries between public, for-profit, and nonprofit sectors. By working closely with the clients and consumers, design thinking allows high-impact solutions to bubble up from below rather than being imposed from the top.[51]

The integration of design, design thinking, and social innovation in product development, marketing, and branding can provide many indigenous peoples with entrepreneurial opportunities. One clear example of indigenous innovation through the combination of *Community, Spirituality, Sustainability,* and *Entrepreneurship* are the branding activities of the Māori people in New Zealand. Harmsworth and Tahi describe in detail the integration of Māori indigenous culture, values, and knowledge in the building of indigenous-branded enterprises that can compete on a global market scale:

> Indigenous branding is being used widely by Māori enterprise and appears well positioned to play a major role for Māori enterprise and Brand NZ (NZTE 2005b) in global markets as long as strategies are robust, based on Māori values, knowledge, and integrity, and follow a set of effective and appropriate guiding principles. . . . The future challenge for most Māori enterprises, as with all indigenous enterprises, is how to balance aspirations for cultural enrichment—which retain and strengthen cultural definition and wellbeing, including values, customary practice, language, technology and knowledge—with aspirations to pursue advancement, growth, commerce, and economic development.[52]

Clearly the Māori have been able to embrace a multitude of factors specific to their indigenous context that ultimately effect positive social, cultural, sustainable, and economic outcomes. In one sense these Māori outcomes can be seen as the product of the decolonized quadruple bottom line, as each of the factors of *Community, Spirituality, Sustainability,* and *Entrepreneurship* has played an important role in their development.

CONCLUSION
[QUADRUPLE BOTTOM LINE AND THE PRODUCTION OF INDIGENOUS INNOVATION]

Izaidin Abdul Majid and Wei-loon Koe in "Sustainable Entrepreneurship (SE): A Revised Model Based on Triple Bottom Line (TBL)" offer a revision to the John Elkington's 1994 definition of the triple bottom line. In addition to Elkington's three principles of economic prosperity, environmental quality, and social justice, Majid and Koe call for the inclusion of a cultural domain in the context of sustainable entrepreneurship. O'Neill, Hershauer, and Golden, in their article "The Cultural Context of Sustainability Entrepreneurship," state that if "sustainability entrepreneurship is going to be a primary vehicle by which the world makes a transition toward sustainability, it will occur in many cultural contexts." In terms of the future, the authors speculate that sustainability entrepreneurship "might include the creation of sustainability ventures in settings that are not currently highly entrepreneurial" and will probably exist in the global marketplace.[53] They conclude by offering a sustainability model based on the traditional Navajo dwelling known as the Hooghan. Here, the authors purport that the four dimensions of *Environment, Social, Economic,* and *Cultural* exist within the realm of the *Spiritual,* emphasizing that the number four is considered sacred in the traditional Navajo belief system.

With respect to the cultural domain offered by Majid and Koe and spiritual domain offered by O'Neill, Hershauer, and Golden, what is needed as part of the indigenous peoples' experience is a move from a triple bottom line to a quadruple bottom line that advances the entrepreneurial efforts of indigenous peoples globally (see Figure 1). As discussed in the previous five sections, the decolonized quadruple bottom line presented in this essay is intended as a framework for developing innovative business strategies within indigenous communities based on the combination of the four factors of *Community, Spirituality, Sustainability,* and *Entrepreneurship* that are unique to indigenous peoples. The decolonized quadruple bottom line is an attempt to build a theoretical decolonized model of indigenous innovation and entrepreneurship from an indigenous/American Indian perspective in which each of the factors of *Community, Spirituality, Sustainability,* and *Entrepreneurship* (including the subfactors of *Cultural, Social, Economic,* and *Environmental*) are essential in the production of *Indigenous Innovation.* It is only through a decolonized quadruple bottom line approach that indigenous innovation can be realized to its fullest potential toward the support of sustainable community and economic development by and for indigenous peoples.

AUTHOR BIOGRAPHIES

John Takamura is associate professor of industrial design in The Design School at the Herberger Institute for Design and the Arts at Arizona State University.

Fonda Walters (Navajo) was formerly the senior research analyst at the American Indian Policy Institute at Arizona State University.

NOTES

1   "Triple Bottom Line," *The Economist,* http://www.economist.com/node/14201663, November 17, 2009; Fonda Walters, "Promoting Entrepreneurship in a Tribal Context: Evaluation of the First Innovations Course Sequence" (PhD diss., Arizona State University, 2012).

2   Linda Tuhiwai Smith, *Decolonizing Methodologies: Research and Indigenous Peoples,* 2nd ed. (New York: Zed Books Ltd., 1999), 39.

3   Heather Marie Layton and Harry Anthony Patrinos, "Estimating the Number of Indigenous People in Latin America," in *Indigenous People, Poverty, and Human Development in Latin America: 1994–2004,* eds. G. Hall and H. A. Patrinos (London: Palgrave Macmillan, 1994), 25–39.

4   Ibid.

5   "World Bank Group's 2005 Operational Policy 4.10," revised April 2013, http://web.worldbank.org/WBSITE/EXTERNAL/PROJECTS/EXTPOLICIES/EXTOPMANUAL/0,,contentMDK:20553653~menuPK:4564187~pagePK:64709096~piPK:64709108~theSitePK:502184~isCURL:Y,00.html.

6   Gregory K. Ingram, *Implementation of Operational Directive 4.20 on Indigenous Peoples: An Independent Desk Review,* 2003, 1.

7   Jeff Corntassel, "Who Is Indigenous? 'Peoplehood' and Ethnonationalist Approaches to Rearticulating Indigenous Identity," *Nationalism and Ethnic Politics* 9, no. 1 (Spring 2003): 75–100.

8   John L. Steckley, *The Eighteenth-Century Wyandot: A Clan-Based Study* (Waterloo, Ont.: Wilfrid Laurier University Press, 2014).

9   G. Witherspoon, *Navajo Kinship and Marriage* (Chicago: Chicago University Press, 1975).

10 Sohail Inayatullah, "Spirituality as the Fourth Bottom Line?," *Futures: The Journal of Policy Planning and Futures Studies* 37 (2005): 573–79.

11 Kurt Alan Ver Beek, "Spirituality: A Development Taboo," *Development in Practice* 10, no. 1 (2000): 31–43.

12 Ibid., 41.

13 Smith, *Decolonizing Methodologies,* 39.

14 Ray Barnhardt and Angayuqaq Oscar Kawagley, "Indigenous Knowledge Systems and Alaska Native Ways of Knowing," *Anthropology and Education Quarterly* 36, no. 1 (2005): 8–23.

15 Keith D. Morrison and Simron J. Singh, "Adaptation and Indigenous Knowledge as a Bridge to Sustainability," *Current Trends*

in *Human Ecology* 125, no. 155 (2009): 125–55.

16 Ibid.

17 Wanda Wuttunee, Mary Jane Loustel, and D. Overall, "Indigenous Values and Contemporary Management Approaches," *The Journal of Aboriginal Economic Development* 5, no. 2 (2007): 20–30.

18 Simon Ortiz, "Sustainability from an Indigenous Perspective" (lecture, Arizona State University, Entrepreneurship for American Indian Sustainability, Spring 2012).

19 Ibid.

20 Wuttunee, Loustel, and Overall, "Indigenous Values," 21.

21 Stephen Cornell and Joe Kalt, "Two Approaches to the Development of Native Nations: One Works, the Other Doesn't," in *Rebuilding Native Nations: Strategies for Governance and Development*, ed. M. Jorgensen (Tucson: University of Arizona Press, 2007), 1–33.

22 Stephen Cornell, "Tribal–Citizen Entrepreneurship: What Does It Mean for Indian Country, and How Can Tribes Support It?" (condensed version of speech presented at the Montana Indian Business Conference, Great Falls, Montana, 2006).

23 Walters, "Promoting Entrepreneurship in a Tribal Context," 29–31.

24 Robert J. Miller, *Reservation "Capitalism": Economic Development in Indian Country* (Santa Barbara, Calif.: Praeger, 2012), 27.

25 David W. Murray, "Self-Sufficiency and the Creation of Dependency: The Case of Chief Isaac Inc.," *American Indian Quarterly* 16 (Spring 1992): 169–88.

26 Miller, *Reservation "Capitalism,"* 28; Richard White, *The Roots of Dependency: Subsistence, Environment, and Social Change among the Choctaws, Pawnees, and Navajos* (Lincoln: University of Nebraska Press, 1983), xvi–xvii; Murray, "Self-Sufficiency and the Creation of Dependency," 171.

27 Brian C. Hosmer, *American Indians in the Marketplace: Persistence and Innovation among the Menominees and Metlakatlans, 1870–1920* (Lawrence: University of Kansas Press, 1999), 1–13, 16; Miller, *Reservation "Capitalism,"* 29.

28 Miller, *Reservation "Capitalism,"* 29; Patricia Albers, "Labor and Exchange in American Indian History," in *A Companion to American Indian History*, eds. Philip Deloria and Neal Salisbury (Malden, Mass.: Blackwell Publishers, 2002), 279.

29 Brian Hosmer and Colleen O'Neill, *Native Pathways: American Indian Culture and Economic Development in the Twentieth Century* (Boulder: University Press of Colorado, 2004), 6–7, 11; Miller, *Reservation "Capitalism,"* 29.

30 Elinor Ostrum, "A General Framework for Analyzing Sustainability of Social-Ecological Systems," *Science* 325 (2009): 419.

31 Ibid., 420.

32 F. Stuart Chapin III, Carl Folke, and Gary P. Kofinas, "A Framework for Understanding Change," in *Principles of Ecosystem Stewardship: Resilience-Based Natural Resource Management in a Changing World*, eds. F. Stuart Chapin III, Carl Folke, and Gary P. Kofinas (New York: Springer, 2009), 3–28.

33 B. L. Turner II, Roger E. Kasperson, Pamela A. Matson, James J. McCarthy, and Robert W. Corell, et al., "A Framework for Vulnerability Analysis in Sustainability Science," *Proceedings of the National Academy of Sciences* (2003); W. Neil

Adger, "Vulnerability," *Global Environmental Change* (2006); Chapin, Folke, and Kofinas, "A Framework for Understanding Change," 22.

34 Carl Folke, "Resilience: The Emergence of Perspective for Social-Ecological Systems Analyses," *Global Environmental Change* 16, no. 3 (2006): 253–67.

35 WCED: The World Commission on Environment and Development, "Our Common Future" (Oxford University Press: New York, 1987).

36 Chapin, Folke, and Kofinas, "A Framework for Understanding Change," 24.

37 Miller, *Reservation "Capitalism,"* 11.

38 Walters, "Promoting Entrepreneurship in a Tribal Context," 9.

39 Ibid., 12.

40 Izaidin Abdul Majid and Wei-Loon Koe, "Sustainable Entrepreneurship (SE): A Revised Model Based on Triple Bottom Line (TBL)," *International Journal of Academic Research in Business and Social Sciences* 2, no. 6 (2012): 293–310.

41 Robert A. Miller and Elizabeth W. Collier, "Redefining Entrepreneurship: A Virtues and Values Perspective," *Journal of Leadership, Accountability, and Ethics* 8, no. 2 (2010): 80–88.

42 Walters, "Promoting Entrepreneurship in a Tribal Context," 33.

43 Anders Abrahamsson, "Sustainopreneurship—Business with a Cause: Conceptualizing Entrepreneurship for Sustainability" (MA thesis, Växjö University, 2007); K. Hockerts and R. Wüstenhagen, "Greening Goliaths versus Emerging Davids: Theorizing about the Role of Incumbents and New Entrants in Sustainable Entrepreneurship," *Journal of Business Venturing* 25, no. 5 (2010): 481–92; D. A. Shepherd and H. Patzelt, "The New Field of Sustainable Entrepreneurship: Studying Entrepreneurial Action Linking 'What Is to Be Sustained' with 'What Is to Be Developed,'" *Entrepreneurship Theory and Practice* (January 2011): 137–63; Gerald Dan O'Neill Jr., J. C. Hershauer, and J. S. Golden, "The Cultural Context of Sustainability Entrepreneurship," *Green Management International* 55 (2009): 33–46.

44 Wuttunee, Loustel, and Overall, "Indigenous Values," 20–30.

45 Stan Metcalfe and Ronnie Ramlogan, "Innovation Systems and the Competitive Process in Developing Economies," *The Quarterly Review of Economics and Finance* 48, no. 2 (2008): 433–46.

46 Metcalfe and Ramlogan, "Innovation Systems and the Competitive Process," 433–46.

47 Renee Stepler, Steve Garguilo, Khanjan Mehta, and Sven Bilen, "Applying Systems Thinking for Realizing the Mission of Technology-Based Social Ventures in Africa," *Proceedings of the ASEE Annual Conference* (Louisville, Ky., 2010).

48 Tim Brown and Jocelyn Wyatt, "Design Thinking for Social Innovation," *Stanford Social Innovation Review* 8, no. 1 (2010): 30–35.

49 Ibid.

50 Tim Brown, "Design Thinking," *Harvard Business Review* (Cambridge Mass.: Harvard Business School Publishing Corp., June 2008).

51 Brown and Wyatt, "Design Thinking for Social Innovation," 32.

52 Garth Harmsworth and Marino Tahi, "Indigenous Branding: Examples from Aotearoa New Zealand" (paper presented at FIBEA, Fostering Indigenous

Business and Entrepreneurship in the Americas conference, Manaus, Brazil, July 22–25, 2008). For the guiding principles referred to by the authors, see Mason H. Durie, *Te Mana, Te Kāwanatanga: The Politics of Māori Self-Determination* (Auckland, NZ: Oxford University Press, 1998), 280.

53 O'Neill Jr., Hershauer, and Golden, "The Cultural Context of Sustainability Entrepreneurship," 38.

Appeals to Civilization and Customary "Forest Diplomacy"

Arguments against Removal in Letters Written by the Iroquois, 1830–1857

Claudia B. Haake

In this essay I argue that in order to try and persuade the U.S. government that it was unnecessary to exile them from their lands in the East to the west of the Mississippi under the removal policy, member tribes of the Haudenosaunee (Iroquois) Confederacy of the northeastern United States had to engage in the discourse of progress toward civilization that white Americans used to justify their policy. In their appeals to U.S. officials, the Iroquois invoked their peoples' progress in agricultural pursuits and the existence of settlements, drawing attention to their progress in religion, morality, and educational achievements. Significantly, however, they did not limit themselves to mounting such an argument focused merely on white American political rhetoric.

Those Iroquois opposed to removal also drew from their own traditions to support their position. They devised a complex and multilayered dialogue with the federal government.[1] A number of their written appeals followed in the tradition of wampum, strings of shell beads that had formerly been an essential element of diplomatic encounters in the Northeast. Iroquois representatives also used kinship terms of address reminiscent of those in use during the heyday of "forest diplomacy," as anthropologist William Fenton and others have called the diplomatic encounters and conventions of the colonial era, which drew in large part on Native American traditions and of which the Iroquois had been masterful exponents.[2] The letters the Iroquois wrote in opposition to removal thus did not simply represent appeals to be spared

WICAZO SA REVIEW

FALL 2015

removal and to remain on their lands, but also constituted Iroquois efforts to renew proper diplomatic relations with the U.S. government and to find compromises between their respective positions, as they had been able to do during the colonial era and into the early days of the white American republic. The senders of these letters continued to practice those impressive diplomatic skills that in the not-so-recent past had forced Euro-Americans to engage with Native diplomatic protocol, while stressing their determination to preserve their customary ways of living.

Even before the onset of their removal crisis, which lasted from the 1830s until well into the 1850s, the Iroquois Confederacy, comprised of the Mohawk, Oneida, Onondaga, Cayuga, Seneca, and Tuscarora, had a long history of land cessions. In particular, the "treaty" of 1826 in which the Senecas under the authority of the federal government ceded all remaining Genesee valley lands to the Ogden Land Company, was controversial for its many irregularities and had cost them vast quantities of land.[3] Through it the Ogden Land Company, which continuously agitated for Indian removal, had gained access to Iroquois lands for which it had previously purchased the preemption rights. A subsequent investigation arranged by President John Quincy Adams provided evidence for fraud, the use of terror of removal to bully Indians into signing, and the duplicity of interpreters. Still, this treaty, which was not ratified by Congress, was never actually rescinded.[4]

Reacting to their dwindling land base, many Iroquois had decided to not permit any further land losses. In spite of this resolve, which seems to have been shared by many, the 1820s to the 1840s brought more such losses, and these served to push the Confederacy to the brink of removal. Yet the majority of the Iroquois never resigned themselves to being completely parted from their ancestral lands. To fight this dreaded fate, the Iroquois, who in the colonial period had not only been considered a dominant power in the Northeast but had also won recognition for their skills in diplomacy, contested removal in a number of ways, including making legal appeals to the U.S. courts.[5] This essay, however, will focus on just one aspect of this multifaceted resistance: what the Iroquois said in the letters they wrote to U.S. officials from the 1830s to the 1850s in opposition to removal.[6]

Native American letters from the removal period have received scant scholarly attention by historians although literary scholars have convincingly interpreted Native American alphabetic writing in terms of traditional communication, such as wampum or bark painting.[7] Indigenous writing has been largely ignored for several reasons, which include an unconscious judgment by scholars that writing was an unspectacular strategy compared to actual fighting or bringing legal suits. Yet, as New Zealand scholar Lyndsey Head has argued, "it may be that colonial chiefliness lies in the courage to continue to engage with the state" and such engagement included writing letters.[8] In addition to scholarly prejudices about indigenous resistance, there has often been a sense that oral history is the only proper way of doing Native American history.[9] This frequently seems to rest on the erroneous assumption that white people produced all written documents prior to the eighteenth and nineteenth centuries. Furthermore, many researchers, literary scholar Lisa Brooks has suggested, seem to have looked upon Native American writing as somehow "inauthentic."[10] "In our longing to find an 'authentic Native voice' speaking to us from the past," Hilary Wyss, another literary scholar, has similarly suggested, "we have ignored those who wrote and thought from a Native perspective that included a sense of their colonial position."[11]

PROGRESS TOWARD CIVILIZATION

In recent studies, scholars such as David Martinez and Philip Round have argued that Native Americans emphasized a shared humanity in their dealings with whites, yet the argument the Iroquois mounted in their letters against removal went beyond this rather simple claim. In about five hundred letters mostly written by men, as individuals or in groups, that were more often than not as well written and grammatically correct and in all practical aspects indistinguishable from those of educated white people, the Iroquois instead criticized the basic assumption behind the removal policy: that removal would aid in what the federal government referred to as their "civilization."[12] They suggested that they could only continue toward this vague idea of civilization if they could remain in place. By doing so they attempted to make use of the discourse that permeated U.S. Indian policy from which the most common argument about progress toward civilization was derived. In order to contradict the contention that their removal would help them to advance toward civilization, the Iroquois found themselves engaged with the U.S. government's lines of reasoning. Thus, their presentations transcended the focus on shared humanity.

The federal government presented civilization as the principal aim of its Indian removal policy. In his second annual message to Congress in December 1830, President Andrew Jackson not only pointed out some of the benefits Indian removal would bring the United States, such as economic advantages and the elimination of conflict between federal and state governments, but he also took pains to highlight the way removal would benefit Native Americans.[13] In doing this he heavily emphasized "civilization." Jackson promised that Indian removal would lead to better use of lands by substituting a "dense and civilized population" for "a few savage hunters" and thus enable Indians to "pursue happiness in their own way." This, Jackson argued, would "perhaps cause them gradually to cast off their savage habits and become an interesting, civilized, and Christian community."[14] Others expressed similar views. For instance, David A. Ogden of the Ogden Land Company—which held the preemption rights, or the right to purchase before the general public has the opportunity, for Iroquois lands—called the Indians half-civilized and half-savage and, like so many others at the time, urged removal for their benefit.[15]

While not everyone within the federal government was convinced by Jackson's arguments or pro-removal policy, the idea of bringing civilization to the Indians was generally accepted among whites. Indians were seen as uncivilized in large part because of the way they used the land. There was an established tradition in Western thought that informed this Eurocentric view. As Ronald Meek has described, from ancient writers onward the idea was often that there was "normal" societal progress, which saw societies move from hunting and gathering to pastoralism and agriculturalism and on to commerce, their final stage of development.[16] In the eighteenth century especially, philosophers of the Scottish school elaborated on this theory, arguing that most human societies developed or progressed through stages; this tradition of thought claimed that indigenous peoples had not reached the agricultural stage. Property rights, Greek and Roman writers had already held, only came with agriculture.[17] This "classical association of agriculture and property in land," as legal scholar Stuart Banner has pointed out, "persisted through the medieval and early modern eras," and it was within this framework that the English understood the Indians and their property rights when they reached the new world.[18]

U.S. settlers used the Indians' alleged lack of civilization to justify the dispossession of the Natives. Indians, white Americans often argued, should surrender the lands they did not use properly so that those places could be taken up by settlers. They were not the first to do so. Agents of English colonization in the seventeenth century had argued that the measure of rightful possession was efficient use, and early settlers fenced in "unoccupied" land.[19] The same argument that only individual land cultivation justified possession later came to be used to legitimize removal, which was held up as a way for Native Americans to become civilized. Those like the Iroquois who were not yet sufficiently civilized to properly possess land were expected to surrender their traditional territory and remove to the frontier where they would supposedly gain the time needed to become fully civilized. The Indians were supposed to integrate themselves into a system of private individual landownership, or disappear from their old lands in another way. In order to so "disappear," they were expected to become civilized. Removal, at least according to the Jackson administration, was intended to advance them toward this goal. Once they had become civilized, the thought went, they would be able to use the substitute lands offered to them under the terms of the removal policy in a civilized manner and thus to truly own them.

A hallmark of civilization was Christianity, and the idea of progress toward civilization was often linked to the adoption of Christianity, as Jackson acknowledged in his 1830 speech when he expressed the hope of turning Indians into Christian communities.[20] Knowledge of Christ, it was held, would lift the curse of savagery that affected the descendants of Noah's son Ham. Efforts by missionaries and others to bring Native Americans to embrace Christianity and a "white" lifestyle, however, were considered to have failed in spite of many Indians having done so at least to an extent, for instance by adopting a different style of agriculture.[21] This type of reasoning allowed U.S. leaders to justify the taking of Indians' lands on the basis of their lack of civilization while also claiming that removal would advance them toward it. Yet, as historian Christopher Tomlins has shown, as time went on English argumentation focused relatively less on the spread of Christianity and more on civilization alone.[22]

The idea of "civilization" so dominated that few nineteenth-century white Americans questioned the assumption that it would be beneficial and desirable for Indians to become "civilized." Many white advocates and opponents of removal simply differed on the best way of achieving this goal, and the Iroquois were well aware of these differing viewpoints. The Iroquois would have gained an understanding of how the policy was justified with the language of civilization, from representations of removal as inevitable and the explanations provided to them by U.S. officials, missionaries, and others who would have supported the goal of becoming civilized.[23]

In seeking to oppose removal, Iroquois leaders emphasized that they had already made considerable progress toward civilization, providing concrete evidence whenever possible in support of their contention. In their correspondence to U.S. officials, the Iroquois, who had always practiced some agriculture (though in accordance with their own gender roles), made reference to how they had advanced in agriculture. In February 1838, some residents of Onondaga Castle emphasized to the House of Representatives and the Senate that they had "made considerable progress in agriculture," and as late as July 1853, Ely S. Parker, identifying himself as head chief of the Tonawanda Senecas, reiterated that "our ancient hunting grounds have been changed into productive farms."[24] Over time, various groups among the Iroquois similarly emphasized material advances in the realm of agriculture, such as the fact that they had "houses and barns, horses + cattle."[25] In July 1853 Parker also laid claim to an advanced degree of civilization by pointing to "thriving villages and cities," which, like agriculture, were associated with civilization.[26] By referring to settlements and especially cities, the Iroquois showed an awareness that towns and cities were considered an important representation of civilization. As Tomlins has explained, villages and cities symbolized ordered and concentrated settlement and were the spatial embodiment of political–legal jurisdiction, and Parker drew on this notion.[27]

In addition to agricultural advances, the Iroquois pointed to progress made in the realm of education. Eighteenth-century European intellectuals viewed education as crucial to the advancement of societies, and many early American leaders, such as Thomas Jefferson, held the same opinion.[28] The task of bringing education to Indians often fell on missionaries. Missionaries, in turn, "considered literacy training a practical method of confirming and disseminating European values."[29] In order to achieve the true conversion they sought for their Indian charges, missionaries held the so-called trappings of civilization to be necessary; therefore, missionaries sought to advance at least some of the goals the government had for the Indians.[30] But the U.S. government also took steps to foster its goals. The Civilization Fund, created by Congress in 1819, aimed to introduce Indians to "the habits and arts of civilization." Future Seneca leader and first Native American Commissioner of Indian Affairs Ely S. Parker repeatedly applied to this fund for school fees.[31] Furthermore, starting in 1820, the federal government specifically set aside portions of Indian annuities, established by treaties, for educational programs within Indian lands. As historian Ronald Satz has indicated, though its subsidized education programs under Andrew Jackson, the federal government pursued the conversion of the Indians from "savages" to "civilized" men.[32]

Such measures made focusing on education logical for Indian letter writers and petitioners, especially as the teachings of Handsome Lake, the relatively recent revitalization movement embraced by many of the authors of written communication to the federal government, encouraged education.[33] Another reason for embracing the white form of education was the realization that it would help them in the defense of Iroquois lands.[34] However, it was much harder for Native Americans to successfully argue that they had advanced in education than it was to show that they had advanced in agriculture, as there was less visible evidence to support such claims. Still, authors of Iroquois letters often pointed to school buildings and to those among them who had acquired "white" skills as the result of European education and other training. In an 1837 letter, for instance, residents of Buffalo Creek informed U.S. President Martin Van Buren that they had built schoolhouses.[35]

In their letters, the Iroquois also made much of the rapid progress in their moral condition by dint of their embrace of Christianity. This focus not only reflected the influence missionaries had had over them, but it also stressed the connection many Americans made between Christianity and civilization, believing that acquiring the latter was dependent on converting to the former.[36] In an 1837 letter, for example, they claimed that their moral condition was improving but admitted that there were still immoral men among their people, arguing that all nations shared this condition.[37] Like progress in education, moral advances were intangible and thus hard to prove. But, whenever possible, letter writers made the most of what evidence there was, such as pointing to church buildings.[38] For instance, in 1843, the Tonawanda Senecas, including ardent anti-removal leader John Blacksmith who had been "raised up" to league chief to replace the deposed pro-emigrationist Little Johnson, told U.S. President John Tyler that they were "now just beginning to adopt the manners & customs of our white neighbors & have erected churches & school houses for the education of our children."[39]

While the Iroquois writers emphasized their progress toward civilization, whether it was in regard to agriculture, education, or morality, they did not merely respond to the dominant discourse favored by white America. Rather, they challenged that discourse by arguing that removal away from civilization would be counterproductive. When constructing the argument that they would be unable to continue progressing toward civilization unless they were to remain on their homelands, the Iroquois writers did not question removal policy as such. They merely stated that it would not work for them as they had already advanced considerably toward civilization. However, they did not dispute that removal might work for others who were less advanced. While in 1837 Buffalo Creek Seneca chiefs told the president that they believed "that our comforts here are better than the Western territory can offer us," Iroquois letter writers also pointed out that they were "not, like the western Indians, wanderers beyond the pale of civilization" and that for this reason the removal policy should not be applied to them.[40]

At the same time that they emphasized their progress and tied its continuation to remaining on their own lands without ever challenging the removal policy in itself, most of the Iroquois letter writers were also careful not to go so far as to claim that they had become completely civilized. The authors seem to have realized that this was not an argument the U.S. government was likely to accept. The Iroquois would also have known that a claim to having reached a stage of civilization equal to that of Euro-Americans would have led to demands for them to become incorporated into the state of New York as individual citizens, something they seemed as eager to avoid as removal.[41] For both these reasons, they stated that they were "neither savages nor a civilized community," that they were "now just beginning to adopt the manners & customs of our white neighbours," and that they could not yet farm like white men.[42]

By pointing to their advances in civilization, particularly in agriculture, education, and morality, the Iroquois did not openly challenge or contest the stated objective of removal policy: civilizing Native Americans. Instead, they questioned its capacity to advance them toward this goal.

WAMPUM AND WRITING

While the Iroquois in their letters opposing removal often adopted a rhetoric about progress toward civilization as this had long been the way the government had justified removal and its broader Indian policy, Iroquois letter writers also incorporated some more traditional elements of Iroquois diplomacy into their correspondence. Some letters draw on methods and symbols that had been employed with much success in the heyday of the "forest diplomacy" of the sixteenth to eighteenth centuries more openly than others, yet even those that on the surface appear to be just highly formal missives by educated men and written in a "white" style frequently contain elements that had once been commonplace at treaty councils. And while the Iroquois did not use all elements of "forest diplomacy" in this different and new medium, they did call on some of them.[43] The "retaining and retelling" of old agreements through the use of wampum, shell bead belts, or strings—which the Confederacy as well as others had formerly utilized in all treaty councils—was one such example of a customary element of "forest diplomacy" that, in modified form, was used by the Iroquois in their letter writing.[44]

In many Iroquois letters written in opposition to removal their authors subtly appealed to traditions of colonial-era "forest diplomacy," where, as Fenton has argued, nothing had more force "than the sanction of ritual and its continued renewal."[45] They often appealed to these rituals by gesturing to the fact that they and their interlocutors had previously negotiated treaties that they still considered to be binding. At times they did this in a manner reminiscent of some of the functions that had once been fulfilled by wampum, which put, as Australian scholar Penny van Toorn has said in another context, "these alien elements . . . within Indigenous frames of reference."[46]

Wampum belts of white and black or purple shell beads had been of the highest importance, especially in treaty councils, and without them what was said could be considered a mere rumor.[47] Thus, for the Iroquois, wampum was "the 'word' or the 'voice' containing messages to be delivered," and it "constituted legal documentation of an act or intent."[48] When it fell out of favor with the colonial powers, some of its functions, as Iroquois correspondence with the federal government shows, came to be at least partly reassigned to letters and petitions. This was the case even though the Iroquois had initially been uncomfortable at the sight of "scribbling" at treaty conferences of old.[49]

Some continued to see writing as a disruption of oral protocol and therefore disliked it, but others among the Confederacy embraced it as a tool readily available to them in their fight against removal.[50] Often writing a letter was the only way to contact the federal government: delegations were expensive and time consuming, and the federal government in 1833 changed its policy and frequently refused to authorize them.[51] The Cherokees, as historian Andrew Denson and others have shown, were particularly adept at using writing in their fight for nationhood.[52] Yet this did not mean that writing came to completely supplant all indigenous systems of communication. Rather, as Lisa Brooks has elucidated, these systems were modified or merged with new ones. "Throughout northeastern networks," Brooks has argued, "writing took on a role that was complementary to that of wampum."[53] This becomes apparent in the letters analyzed here, which, as Brooks has contended for Native petitions, can be seen as a genre unto themselves.[54] These letters, I suggest, are attempts at finding a compromise between the Iroquois and the government, through drawing on traditions of the colonial era or the early republic.

Even in the colonial period, the Iroquois at times treated letters much like wampum. Letters were stored with wampum, held up, and "talked to" or addressed like wampum. Letters with strings attached to them, according to some reports, particularly were seen as similar to wampum by members of the Confederacy.[55] Only thirty years prior to the onset of the Iroquois removal crisis, Treaty Commissioner Timothy Pickering reported to Secretary of War Henry Knox that the Iroquois treated documents with ribbons attached as though they were wampum belts.[56] The two mediums, wampum and letters, seem to have been regarded by the Iroquois as having at the very least similar functions, even though the Iroquois thought wampum had a decided advantage over writing as it required some face-to-face interaction, which they favored. Wampum contained messages or recorded agreements, and belts could be grasped or refused, which made them a more direct as well as subtle instrument of diplomacy than letters, sent without accompanying messengers over vast distances, could ever be. Furthermore, wampum was not only regarded as a sacred substance, it was also a valuable commodity; its use underscored that the speaker was not just talking for himself but had the support of others. Writing, on the other hand, as the Iroquois knew only too well, could be filled with empty promises and was thus seen as less reliable by some members of the Confederacy.[57] Nonetheless, once wampum had fallen out of favor with Euro-Americans, and many other aspects of "forest diplomacy" had disappeared, the Iroquois were forced to turn to writing for their diplomatic dealings with the U.S. government.

Wampum was also a mnemonic device that helped speakers to recall the details of an agreement. It could be brought out again and again, the periodic reiteration ensuring that the accord was remembered and thus honored. It is this function of "retaining and retelling" an agreement—first recalling and then reminding the other party of promises made, obligations entered into, and maintenance required by both sides—which the Iroquois in some of their letters to the government incorporated in a novel manner. This customary function of wampum, which, as Brooks has described, made sure that spoken words were honored and agreements remembered, was also a means by which the letter writers were able to remind the federal government of promises made in treaties that had supposedly been permanent and ask it to live up to these assurances.[58] Here "white" and "red" practices were not all that dissimilar, and letters thus were a way of engaging in a multilayered dialogue that could be read in both systems.

The agreement to which Iroquois letter writers most often referred in this retaining and retelling mode was the 1794 Treaty of Canandaigua, negotiated for the federal government by future Secretary of War Timothy Pickering. As historian Matthew Dennis has argued, the treaty "seemed to affirm both [President George] Washington's authority and his benevolence," and the latter was something many letters of the removal era especially emphasized. The treaty also "seemed to have won federal affirmation of [Seneca] sovereignty and federal protection against acquisitive and duplicitous land companies."[59] Historian Laurence Hauptman has similarly pointed to the importance of the Treaty of Canandaigua in Iroquois conceptions of their own sovereignty, which they felt the United States had recognized through that accord when "both parties exchanged assurances of perpetual friendship while the United States gave a guarantee of territorial integrity."[60] The 1794 treaty also described the boundaries of the Confederacy's lands.

The importance the Iroquois attached to the treaty was obvious in the letters they wrote to the federal government in an attempt to avoid removal. In this correspondence, the Iroquois invoked the treaty in order to emphasize continued commitment to it in a manner that was reminiscent of the ways in which they might have talked about the colonial-era "covenant chain," a friendship agreement that needed to be regularly "polished," for instance by gift giving, in order to remain valid. For example, in October 1837 the Buffalo Creek Seneca chiefs, in one of their many letters, alluded to this treaty of peace, stating that they still adhered to the forty-year-old agreement.[61] And during a council in 1840, an Allegany chief told the government representative present that they still held to the treaty made with the Great Father in Washington, which they claimed guaranteed their possession of their "lands as long as grass grows and water runs."[62] In 1849, members of the reservation including Jemmy Johnson, who had become one of Tonawanda's major spokesman after Red Jacket's death, and John Blacksmith, who seems to have taken over this role in the mid-1840s, appealed to the treaties "by which the lands had been guaranteed to them forever."[63] They again mentioned this treaty guarantee of their lands in an 1850 letter to the secretary of the Interior and also invoked it in one to the president in 1853, describing it as the treaty made many winters ago with Great Father George Washington.[64] Whether specifically, like in appeals to the Treaty of Canandaigua, or more generally, as when they invoked the colonial-era diplomatic concept of the covenant chain, many times Iroquois tried to make letters fill the function of retelling historical agreements, formerly one of the tasks of wampum.

In several of the letters sent by them, Iroquois also used a wampum-like approach when it came to providing an account of history, something literary scholar Maureen Konkle argues can be interpreted as an extension of Iroquois political tradition.[65] "At councils to renew the peace," as historian Nancy Shoemaker has explained, "it was vital to recount the history of the alliance."[66] This retelling at one time would have been linked to wampum belts, which helped the speakers to recall the events. On such occasions, belts were held up while past agreements and their history were recited. The Iroquois, following the conventions of "forest diplomacy," retained these belts and periodically brought them out to recite the history of past interactions and agreements. As Hauptman has indicated in his discussion of Blacksmith of Tonawanda, some of the old chiefs had a great knowledge of history, even though they may not have been able to read or write English.[67]

In their letters, which were in many ways substitutes for diplomatic councils, Iroquois writers at times still followed diplomatic customs, and these letters are among the most traditional-looking examples of all their correspondence with the federal government. One of these was sent from the president of the newly created Seneca Nation to Secretary of the Interior Thomas Ewing in November 1849. In it, the authors also utilized other protocols of forest diplomacy, such as kinship forms of address. While Ewing was addressed as "brother" throughout, the letter's author also referred to the "Great Father the President" and to "his red Children," the Iroquois.[68] The letter resembled the customs associated with wampum in its speech-like retelling of the history of the interactions between the Iroquois and the United States. The retelling in the letters resembled treaty councils where a speech would have been supported by wampum belts as visible reminders and mnemonic devices. Another example of letters being used in the tradition of wampum can be found in an 1855 one to Commissioner of Indian Affairs George W. Manypenny from Cattaraugus Senecas. In this missive, the authors looked back on their history with white people and referred to the chain of friendship, also known as the covenant chain, an important metaphor from the time of forest diplomacy. In the letter, the authors created a speech-like pattern through stylized repetition, repeatedly asking its recipient to "listen while the Senecas speak," and using "brother" to address him, much as if the commissioner had been present at an actual council.[69]

Federal promises about the permanence of treaties enabled Iroquois to demand that past assurances would be honored. They way in which they expressed their demands overlapped with their customary ideas about maintenance of such agreements and were reminiscent of former uses of wampum. But this was not the only element of forest diplomacy that can be found in Iroquois letters to the federal government during the removal era.

FORMS OF ADDRESS

While in the majority of their removal-era correspondence the Iroquois authors adopted a mostly "white" and "civilized" style of writing, they still went beyond what anthropologist Thomas Abler has somewhat offhandedly referred to as "aping" another society's letter-writing format. For instance, they included customary forms of kinship address in their letters, often consciously, it would seem.[70] Not only was fictional kinship the basis of the League of the Iroquois, but during the colonial era kinship metaphors also had been one of the organizing principles of diplomatic interactions between northeastern Native Americans and Europeans.[71] The use of kinship forms of address continued throughout the Iroquois removal crisis, during which the letter writers used such forms in addressing their correspondents in about a quarter of all the letters written to the federal government.[72]

Iroquois authors especially used the terms "father" or "great father." While there is some question about the way the figure of the father had been seen in precontact matrilineal Iroquois society, one might speculate that because the father in a matrilineal society is less important than the maternal uncle, it was likely not considered degrading for the Iroquois to refer to the colonizer as their "father." Still, there seems to be no doubt that the Iroquois soon came to comprehend at least some of what the Europeans had in mind when they used the term, because it appears that the kinship address of "father" for the Iroquois went in a relatively short time from one rooted in their own society and culture and tied mostly to their own expectations, to one of the ever-shifting and constantly negotiated "middle ground" in which forest diplomacy took place.[73] By the removal era, if not long before, government officials had also come to habitually use this terminology and regularly addressed tribal leaders on behalf of their "father" in Washington.[74]

Letters were at times addressed simply as "Father," while at other times more elaborately, "To our Father the President of the United States."[75] Through the content of some of the letters using this form of address, it becomes clear that the senders felt that someone addressed as "father" should live up to certain standards of behavior derived from

Iroquois customs. Sometimes, like in an 1846 example signed among others by John Blacksmith of Tonawanda, the authors hinted at paternal duties of the president, whom they referred to as "father," and asked explicitly for his protection.[76] At other times, Iroquois letter writers cast themselves in the role of children in order to make such a request for protection implicitly. One such missive from Seneca chiefs explained that they had "taken little steps leaning upon the strong arm of our Father," but were afraid that "our Great Father forgets how young his Seneca children are."[77] Here, the traditional patience expected from a father in Iroquois society, but also familiar to those from other cultural backgrounds and especially to Christians, was asked of the president.

Letter writers did not necessarily always draw merely on one kind of address but frequently mixed customary and new "white" styles. In August 1837, Onondaga chiefs wrote to the president as "Dear Sir, Great Father."[78] A letter dated June 19, 1840, was formally addressed "to His Excellency John Tyler, President of the United States," but in the letter itself the authors repeatedly called the president "Father."[79] Another letter, dated March 1841 and signed by highly respected Governor Blacksnake, among others, referred to the president as "Respected Father, Sir"; another one was addressed, again, "To His Excellency John Tyler President of the United States," yet referred to the president as "Father" throughout the letter.[80] The senders of this latter one signed as "Your Brothers," perhaps aiming to tone down the sometimes-deferential character of the letter as in Iroquois society the relationship among brothers was one of degrees of equality.[81] Iroquois authors again paired traditional and modern forms of address when in 1843 the chiefs of the Tonawanda and Buffalo Creek reservations addressed their letter "to our Father (the President)" and continued to refer to him in this manner, while calling themselves "Your red children."[82]

In addition to drawing on the language of forest diplomacy dating back to the colonial era, and to the role of father in it, letter writers of the Confederacy sometimes also demonstrated an awareness of ideas of paternalism under United States Indian law. At times these two concepts overlapped. For instance, in an 1844 letter from Buffalo Creek chief and warriors to President Tyler, in which the senders addressed him as "Great Father," they hinted at the way this paternal role should have been fulfilled properly under Iroquois customary law, but also linked this role to their new legal status under the Supreme Court's *Cherokee v. Georgia* decision of 1831.[83] According to this ruling, the legal status of Native Americans vis-à-vis the United States resembled that of wards to a guardian. "The law," the chiefs wrote, "declares us to be in the condition of children, and we expected the indulgence and kindness due to that character, so long as we are not willfully [sic] in the wrong."[84] In this letter, the Iroquois authors combined old and new concepts of paternalism and used them to plead for the protection they sought. Sometimes Iroquois writers also tried to utilize this new form of legal paternalism in their fight against land loss and removal without necessarily combining it with their own customary understanding. For instance, in an 1840 petition the authors specifically referred to the president as their guardian, implicitly asking him to live up to this status.[85]

While most letters, including ones that at first glance appear to have been written in the "white" style of the times, utilized some traditional elements of forest diplomacy, only very few did this when they were also pointing out the progress the Iroquois had made toward civilization.[86] Yet such combined appeals were not necessarily incompatible in the eyes of the Iroquois, or at least not to some of them. Among the relatively few letters in which the authors simultaneously invoked the discourse of making progress toward civilization and used traditional forms of kinship address was one of the many written by the Tonawanda chiefs, probably the most outspoken of all Iroquois opponents of removal. In this 1843 letter, the authors addressed the president as "Dear Father, President of the United States" and used "Dear Father" several times in the body of the letter, while also talking about the progress they had made toward civilization and even providing examples of and evidence for their advances.[87] It appears that they saw no contradiction between pointing to progress while using traditional kinship forms of address that may have appeared rather uncivilized to the addressees in the U.S. government—even though government officials not infrequently used such terms themselves, albeit presumably rather condescendingly. Alternatively, casting themselves in the role of children may have constituted an appeal to the colonizer's assumption that the Iroquois were (like) children and a request to be treated with the corresponding kindness and patience that missionaries would have preached as paternal duties among Christians.

Yet the figure of the father had never been the only kinship metaphor of forest diplomacy, even though in recognition of its importance historian Richard White has referred to it as "the master metaphor of the middle ground."[88] Examples of another form of kinship address, namely that of "brother" or "brethren," can also be found in diplomatic interactions in the colonial era.[89] There was a marked difference between this sort of address and the paternal metaphor, as among Iroquois brothers were fundamentally equals, and none of the obedience that elders such as fathers or uncles could expect applied in this kin relationship.[90] Favoring this type of address sent a clear signal, one that Europeans at least initially seemed to have understood since it also reflected Christian understandings. Yet over time the term "father" still came to be the dominant form of address of forest diplomacy.[91] Famous Seneca chief Cornplanter, as historian Daniel Richter has pointed out, believed the shift from "brother" to "father" was prompted by the changing power relations between Indians and colonizers.[92] Richter argues that after the Treaty of Greenville of 1796, "the presidency of the United States settled into the ceremonial role of 'Great Father' to the Indian 'Children' with whom the government made treaties."[93] However, a closer examination of Iroquois correspondence from the years of the removal crisis reveals that both types of kinship address were still (or possibly once again) in use from the 1830s to the 1850s.

Similar to "father," the Iroquois used "brother" in a number of different ways, and sometimes as a regular form of address. For example a group of Iroquois used "Dear brother" in their 1851 letter to Commissioner of Indian Affairs Charles Mix.[94] As with "father," Iroquois letter writers at times combined the term "brother" with other allusions to protocols of forest diplomacy, such as instructions on what was—or was not—proper under Iroquois customary law. One such letter, dating from October 1843, was signed by Jemmy Johnson, John Blacksmith, and others of Tonawanda and addressed to the secretary of war, to whom they referred as "brother" throughout the letter.[95] They explained this form of address to him by stating, "I say Brother because I feel so in my heart," seemingly expressing feelings of affection or possibly hinting at their equality to their correspondent.[96]

The Tonawanda chiefs, prolific letter writers in opposition to land loss and removal, used the term "brother" in a letter from 1843, which they signed "Your Brothers (Chiefs of Tonawanda)."[97] A letter sent from Tonawanda in August 1844 in which the senders insisted on a more equal relationship through the kin terminology chosen, addressed Secretary of War William Wilkins as "brother" and was signed "Your Brothers."[98] In it the senders also referred to the president as father when they reminded Wilkins of the "acres of lands that have been guaranteed to us by our Great Father the President of the United States and his council."[99] At the same time that referring to the "Great Father the President" invoked the obligation of paternal care for them in a traditional way, addressing the secretary as "brother" seemed to indicate that the Tonawanda Seneca chiefs by no means felt subordinate to this official but rather saw their relationship as one of equals. Another letter written by the Tonawanda chiefs in 1843 and addressed in a very formal way to "his Excellency John C. Spencer Secretary of War" was signed "your Red Brothers."[100]

While the kinship address of "brother" usually seems to have been reserved for people other than the president, an 1844 letter from the Buffalo Creek chiefs to President Tyler rather unusually addressed the president himself as "brother," implying an equality that the Iroquois had not insisted on in any prior correspondence during the years of the removal crisis, and quite possibly actively defying the expectation of the government in this respect. This letter was witnessed by the educated but still teenaged Ely S. Parker, who served as a "runner" for the chiefs, by, among other things, helping them with their correspondence.[101]

In general, the Iroquois appear to have been keenly aware of who they were writing to and often chose their form of address accordingly, usually showing a deference to the president that they did not necessarily accord to other U.S. officials.[102] They also used the term "friend," though it seems to have been reserved for those letters that were addressed to Quakers, among whom this form of address would have been common. While the number of kinship letters—about a hundred in total—was not insignificant, in the vast majority of the missives written to the government during the removal crisis the Iroquois made no use of any form of kinship address and instead addressed correspondence simply "Sir" or "Dear Sir" or wrote petition style without any form of direct address. Similarly, they concluded the great majority of letters with expressions such as "Yours" or "Yours sincerely" and in terms of style not only conformed to "white" standards and conventions of correspondence, but usually wrote in clear and grammatical English with no or very few spelling errors or other mistakes. This, I will argue shortly, may have been so by conscious decision to appear "civilized" or might have been the result of the processes by which the letters were composed.

As seen above, the content even of these "civilized" letters, however, was not necessarily devoid of customary Iroquois elements. And in many such letters, as I have shown elsewhere, Iroquois authors also invoked their customary laws.[103] Senders saw no inherent contradiction in combining these elements; alternatively, such pairings may possibly have been due to the way the letters were composed.

LETTER-WRITING PROCESSES

Even when they were not directly or indirectly talking about their progress toward civilization, Iroquois letter writers often made a conscious or subconscious effort to conform to certain norms of what was considered "civilized" by following particular conventions of letter writing. These could include the form of address chosen, the way the letters were phrased, and the closing. While at times such choices were probably consciously made, the fact that Iroquois letter writers followed such conventions may also have been due to the scribes who committed the messages to paper, or to the way the letters were created and specifically the ways in which their content was determined.

Though the content of the letters may have been determined by others, such as councils or chiefs, scribes may have consciously or unconsciously chosen to replicate certain norms and phrases that they had been taught to use in letters by their white or white-educated teachers.[104] As literary scholar Laura J. Murray has determined, replicating norms was what the Indian students of Eleazar Wheelock, the founder of Dartmouth College, did.[105] At the time, instruction in letter writing generally seems to have been conducted via textbooks or manuals with "skeleton letters," or examples that would have supplied a fairly rigid form as a guide for pupils.[106] It is feasible that Iroquois scribes followed such a skeleton as much as possible when writing the letters they were tasked with. It is also possible that the form of address may not have been included in the brief the scribes were given by those Iroquois who determined the content of the letters and that therefore they might have chosen to frame the letters according to what they had been taught was acceptable. This could easily have been the case, especially when letters originated as speeches or discussions but were then committed to paper by an educated person, possibly a "runner," such as Ely S. Parker. Parker, in his private correspondence, was quite critical of some of the chiefs, and he may have tried to subtly influence the letters he wrote on their behalf in order to make them more acceptable to the federal government by making them appear more "civilized," for instance through the form of address used.[107] Other scribes, such as Dartmouth-educated Maris B. Pierce, may well have done the same.[108]

It seems that many letters were often the result of discussions among the Iroquois about the content of their message to the federal government, and possibly the form it should take. In *Letter Writing as a Social Practice*, David Barton and Nigel Hall have called attention to the practice of collective letter writing in some cultures, and for the Iroquois the production of a letter to the federal government often seems to have been such a collective undertaking.[109] Letters might have originated in meetings or councils or on occasion as individual speeches presented to such bodies and thus at times mirror the tensions between individual and collective voices.[110] For instance, the removal-era letter in which the Iroquois authors most openly drew on traditions from the heyday of forest diplomacy was written in 1849 by the president of the Seneca Nation, itself created only the year before, and was intended for the U.S. war secretary. Addressing the war secretary as "brother," the sender stated that "Our Great Father the President of the United States has seen fit to place all his red Children under your care."[111] Through the regular and stylized interspersing of the kinship address of "brother," the author of this letter created a pattern very much reminiscent of the Iroquois speeches for which records survive from the colonial period.[112] One might speculate that this letter originated as a speech that was only later committed to paper and sent under the name of the Seneca Nation's president, who may or may not have been the original speaker as even chiefs had formerly drawn on the services of orators, and this practice may well have continued.[113]

Another letter that probably originated as a speech was sent in 1849 from Seneca chiefs to President James K. Polk, in which they repeatedly implored him to "Listen, Father!"[114] The regular use of this exhortation, paired with the kinship term of father, was again reminiscent of a speech from the era of forest diplomacy, when speeches would have been exchanged over a council fire.[115] Two similar examples, both from the 1850s, show that this type of writing, which one might say combined literacy with orality, persisted throughout the removal crisis. In an 1851 letter, the "Committee of safety [sic] Seneca Nation of Indians" addressed President Millard Fillmore as both "Great Father" and "Father," the latter in a recurring and speech-like pattern.[116] They also used some expressions—such as, "This is all we have to say at present"—that may have been derived from forest diplomacy, in which strict rules existed for what could be talked about when and for how long.[117] Another aspect reminiscent of forest diplomacy in this letter was that the senders of this missive referred to themselves as the president's "red children." And an 1853 letter from Cattaraugus residents who also identified as "red children" to the (unnamed) president was again penned in a speech-like pattern and interspersed with the kinship address "father," clearly drawing on elements of intercultural face-to-face forest diplomacy while following a traditional speech pattern.[118]

One reason that speeches sometimes were turned into letters can at least in part be found in Iroquois custom. Speeches given in the realm of forest diplomacy not only had to persuade the other side but also had to be based on an internal consensus. Letters, while ultimately intended for a white audience, similarly had to persuade a local Iroquois community that usually determined, or at least had to approve, the content of the missive. This aim at multiple audiences, a local Iroquois and a white federal one, as well as the fact that traditionally the chiefs or influential men were respected elders who might have adhered to certain traditions more strongly than younger Iroquois who had some "white" education, may have been responsible for those very traditional elements that can still be found in a number of the letters. This generally—though not exclusively—seems to have been in cases where the letter was signed by several people.[119] Even though there may have been some deviation from the old practice of discussing all matters of importance in council until a consensus was reached, the nature of many of the Iroquois letters to the federal government thus indicates a strong possibility of continuing joint deliberations about the contents of such letters.[120] Many of the letters sent to the government may have been negotiated in this way and thus provide tentative glimpses into the views of nonliterate members of the Confederacy, although it is difficult to isolate the opinions of individuals within them, especially as they often may have been given shape and translated by educated Iroquois scribes.[121]

While at times it seems to have been educated Iroquois scribes who made letters appear more "civilized" in terms of their format, it is clear from the extensive focus on civilization that they were not the only ones to judge Iroquois progress to be an important argument in their favor. This focus on progress toward civilization, be it overt or implied, conscious or unconscious, which generally dominated the letters, made sense given that the U.S. government had stated that it wanted to re-settle Indians in order to give them more time to gradually become civilized. As the U.S. government and others portrayed civilization as the ultimate and central objective of the policy, one of the ways of fighting it was for the Iroquois to argue that they already civilized and thus removal was pointless.

Yet while the Iroquois had indeed advanced a lot toward white standards of civilization, it had not been all that long since the era of diplomatic compromises had ended, and some members of the tribe who contributed to the letters to the federal government would have remembered the waning days of forest diplomacy very well and would have been shaped by this period to an extent. Influential Seneca leader Governor Blacksnake of Allegany, for instance, had been born around the middle of the eighteenth century. Even though he probably was not serving as a leader in Seneca affairs during much of the removal crisis, "he still appears to have been important and recognized in the local community," as Abler has determined.[122] While in the heyday of the for-est diplomacy of the previous century Blacksnake had been too young for a leading role in council, he would have been, like all men who as-pired to leadership roles, learning by observing.[123] And he and others like him, one might speculate, would have brought these expectations about what it had meant to be a leader to bear on their contributions to letters to the federal government. Even younger Iroquois would have heard about the days of forest diplomacy and so their expectations and thinking still would have been shaped by this period to a degree. Therefore, through many of their letters to the federal government the Iroquois appealed in traditional ways to have their demands heard and negotiated, just as they had done in encounters of forest diplomacy.

This was more than longing for a return to a golden age. Even recently there had been examples of something of a tentative accep-tance of Iroquois customs and thus of what one might call remnants of a middle ground. As I have shown elsewhere, the many examples of correspondence referring to Iroquois customary law constituted an en-deavor to make the federal government respect these laws.[124] This was not an altogether unrealistic expectation at the time. As legal historian Lisa Ford has shown, just prior to the removal era a state of legal plural-ism had existed, which saw the parallel running of indigenous and settler legal systems. This dual system had only recently come under pressure.[125] For the Iroquois this would have been illustrated by the case of Tommy Jemmy in the decade before the passage of the Indian Removal Act. In response to an 1822 charge of murder against Seneca chief Tommy

Jemmy for having executed a Seneca woman convicted as a witch, New York State passed a law claiming jurisdiction over all crimes within its borders, thus denying the Senecas' assertion of sovereignty. Yet the legislature also opted to pardon Jemmy and thus avoided antagonizing the Iroquois further.[126]

Given this outcome in the legal realm, perhaps the Iroquois had reason to believe that other such compromises in the tradition of forest diplomacy might still be negotiated. These appeals to civilization as well as customary elements can probably be attributed to a number of factors, including the ways in which the letters were composed and written as well as their authorship. However, the references to what may at least on the face of it appear to be contradictory claims were more than accidental and on occasion even constituted a deliberate strategy on the part of the Haudenosaunee authors of written communications in opposition to removal. It may have been a way of signaling that the two in Iroquois eyes were not mutually exclusive, and that it was up to the Haudenosaunee themselves to decide how they should be weighted.

CONCLUSION

By writing letters to the federal government the Iroquois drew on writing as a tool that both signaled and explained their progress toward civilization but also incorporated elements of older customs such as wampum, kinship forms of address, or speeches. Regardless of whether these elements were included through conscious choices made by the Iroquois or through tensions between individual and collective voices in joint deliberations, this puts writing in the tradition of older forms of Iroquois diplomacy. Like other Indians who referred to papers as "written talks," the Iroquois recognized the resemblance between speaking and writing and used it in many different ways, from straightforward appeals under "white" or "red" conventions to multilayered and complex ones that could be read in different ways.[127]

The authors of Iroquois letters to the federal government used writing as a tool even though it was something, as historian Inga Clendinnen has argued in the Australian colonial context, that whites often seemed to claim for themselves.[128] This white attitude of claiming ownership of writing still appears to prevail in contemporary doubts about the authenticity of Native American writing through the sometimes single-minded scholarly focus on oral history and oral traditions. Literary scholar Christopher Teuton sees this "reification and nostalgia for Native oral traditions . . . as a fulfilment of the West's logocentric desires."[129] The resulting one-sided scholarship has obscured, as Native scholar Robert Warrior has argued, that "the history of Native writing constitutes an intellectual tradition."[130] The letters analyzed here and their authors' efforts to renew proper diplomatic relations between Iroquois and the United States form an important part of this tradition.

When writing to the federal government to oppose their proposed removal, the Iroquois appealed to some of the elements of the "forest diplomacy" of old. But the federal government was extremely reluctant to accept Iroquois arguments regardless of whether they were modeled on United States rhetoric of progress toward civilization, Iroquois customs of forest diplomacy, or constituted more complex and multilayered appeals to both systems. The "middle ground" of the forest diplomacy of the colonial era had been premised on both sides making compromises and signaling how far they would be willing to go in order to do so. Yet it appears that during the removal crisis only the Iroquois were showing such a readiness to compromise by displaying a willingness to adopt aspects of what the federal government and others referred to as civilization while through their letters also subtly insisting on retaining some of their own traditions. Until it permitted the Tonawanda Senecas to buy back some of their lands lost through the treaties of 1838 and 1842, the government in its actions clearly indicated that it was unwilling to compromise on Iroquois removal. While the Iroquois in their letters were appealing for a compromise that would allow them to be a civilized yet tribal people in their old homelands, this was exactly what many in the United States did not want to accept.

AUTHOR BIOGRAPHY

Claudia B. Haake is a senior lecturer in history at La Trobe University, Melbourne. She is author of *The State, Removal, and Indigenous Peoples in the United States and Mexico, 1620–2000* (2007) and coeditor of *Removing Peoples: Forced Migration in the Modern World* (2009).

NOTES

Thanks to Bain Attwood, Katie Holmes, Robert Kenny, and Patrick Wolfe for reading and commenting on drafts of this essay, as well as to Kevin J. White for his very generous suggestions.

1   See Robert A. Williams Jr., *Linking Arms Together: American Indian Treaty Visions of Law and Peace, 1600–1800* (New York and London: Routledge, 1999).

2   See William N. Fenton, *The Great Law and the Longhouse: A Political History of the Iroquois Confederacy* (Norman: University of Oklahoma Press, 1998), 299. Others who have used the term include such historians as Francis Jennings, James Merrell, and Daniel Richter. Recently, it has been criticized as a minimization of Haudenosaunee diplomatic skills. However, in my estimation, whatever the original intention behind the term may have been, it aptly describes that the Iroquois were so skilled in diplomacy that Euro-Americans had to engage with and accept parts of their rituals. See, for instance, Jon Parmenter, *The Edge of the Woods, Iroquoia, 1534–1701* (East Lansing: Michigan State University Press, 2010), 90.

The fact that many of these encounters took place in a forest in my estimation does not detract from the skill level of Haudenosaunee diplomats.

3 See Mary Conable, "A Steady Enemy: The Ogden Land Company and the Seneca Indians" (PhD diss., University of Rochester, 1995).

4 See Laurence Hauptman, *The Tonawanda Senecas' Heroic Battle against Removal: Conservative Activist Indians* (Albany: State University of New York Press, 2011), 150–65; and Hauptman, *Conspiracy of Interests: Iroquois Dispossession and the Rise of New York State* (Syracuse, N.Y.: Syracuse University Press, 1999), 152–56.

5 See Hauptman, *Tonawanda*, and Granville Ganter, "Red Jacket and the Decolonization of Republican Virtue," *American Indian Quarterly* 31, no. 4 (2007): 559–81.

6 The threat of removal actually predated the Indian Removal Act but for the Iroquois Confederacy it became acute with the 1838 Treaty of Buffalo Creek.

7 See Rebecca Earle, "Introduction: Letters, Writers, and the Historian," in *Epistolary Selves: Letters and Letter-Writers, 1600–1945*, ed. Rebecca Earle (Aldershot, U.K.: Ashgate, 1999), 3. A notable exception among the historians is Andrew Denson, *Demanding the Cherokee Nation: Indian Autonomy and American Culture 1830–1900* (Lincoln: University of Nebraska Press, 2004). For writing taking over from Native traditions, see Lisa Brooks, *The Common Pot: The Recovery of Native Space in the Northeast* (Minneapolis: University of Minnesota Press, 2008); Christopher B. Teuton, *Deep Waters* (Lincoln: University of Nebraska Press, 2010); and Nancy Shoemaker, *A Strange Likeness: Becoming Red and White in Eighteenth-Century North America* (Oxford: Oxford University Press, 2004), 10.

8 Lyndsey Head, "Wiremu Tamihana and the *Mana* of Christianity," in *Christianity, Modernity, and Culture: New Perspectives on New Zealand History*, ed. John Stenhouse (Hindmarsh, South Australia: ATF, 2005), 83. This echoes an argument made by Richard White in "Using the Past: History and Native American Studies," in *Studying Native America: Problems and Prospects*, ed. Russell Thornton (Madison: University of Wisconsin Press, 1998), 227.

9 For criticisms of the oral history approach in Native studies, see for instance R. David Edmunds, "Blazing New Trails or Burning Bridges: Native American History Comes of Age," *The Western Historical Quarterly* 39, no. 1 (2008): 14, or Jace Weaver, "More Light Than Heat: The Current State of Native American Studies," *American Indian Quarterly* 31 (Spring 2007): 238.

10 For a discussion of such a perceived lack of authenticity, see Brooks, *Common Pot*, xxxi.

11 Hilary E. Wyss, *Writing Indians: Literacy, Christianity, and Native Community in Early America* (Amherst: University of Massachusetts Press, 2000), 3. See also David Martinez, ed., *The American Indian Intellectual Tradition* (Ithaca, N.Y.: Cornell University Press, 2011), xii.

12 See Martinez, *Tradition*, ix and Phillip H. Round, *Removable Type: Histories of the Book in Indian Country, 1663–1880* (Chapel Hill: University of North Carolina Press, 2010), 145.

13 Andrew Jackson, Second Annual Address to Congress, *The American Presidency Project*, http://www.presidency.ucsb.edu/ws/index.php?pid=29472#axzz1QWTFi3jn.

14 Ibid.

15 See Hauptman, *Tonawanda*, 16.

16 See Ronald L. Meek, *Social Science and the Ignoble Savage* (Cambridge, Mass.: Cambridge University Press, 1976), 2–4.

17 Stuart Banner, *How the Indians Lost Their Land: Law and Power on the Frontier* (Cambridge, Mass., and London: Belknap Press, 2005), 36.

18 Ibid.

19 See Christopher Tomlins, *Freedom Bound: Law, Labor, and Civic Identity in Colonizing English America, 1580–1865* (Cambridge, Mass.: Cambridge University Press), 2010, 144; and Banner, *How the Indians*, 31.

20 See, for instance, David Spadafora, *The Idea of Progress in Eighteenth-Century Britain* (New Haven, Conn.: Yale University Press, 1990); Meek, *Social Science;* Bernard Sheehan, *Savagism and Civility: Indians and Englishmen in Colonial Virginia* (Cambridge, Mass.: Cambridge University Press, 1980); Robert F. Berkhofer, *The White Man's Indian* (New York: Vintage, 1978); Roy Harvey Pearce, *The Savages of America: A Study of the Indian and the Idea of Civilization* (Baltimore, Md.: Johns Hopkins University Press, 1965); Robert A. Williams, *Savage Anxieties: The Invention of Western Civilization* (New York: Palgrave, 2012).

21 See especially Robert F. Berkhofer, *Salvation and the Savage: An Analysis of Protestant Missions and American Indian Response, 1787–1862* (New York: Atheneum, 1972).

22 Tomlins, *Freedom Bound*, 142.

23 See Hauptman, *Conspiracy*, 147.

24 Captain Anliager and others of Onondaga Castle to Senate and House of Representatives, February 1838, M234/583, Na-

tional Archives (NARA). Ely S. Parker, Head chief and representative of the Six Nations, to Commissioner of Indian Affairs George W. Manypenny, July 18, 1853, M234/588, NARA. (This self-description as head chief was inaccurate as Parker was not *Tadobado*). All spelling in this essay is as in the originals, unless otherwise indicated.

25 Captain Anliager and others of Onondaga Castle to Senate and House of Representatives, February 1838, M234/583, NARA.

26 Ibid. Ely S. Parker, Head chief and representative of the Six Nations, to Commissioner of Indian Affairs George W. Manypenny, July 18, 1853, M234/588, NARA.

27 See Tomlins, *Freedom Bound*, 140–49.

28 See Spadafora, *Progress*, especially 176, 252.

29 Steven W. Hackel and Hilary E. Wyss, "Print Culture and the Power of Native Literacy in California and New England Missions," in *Native Americans, Christianity, and the Reshaping of the American Religious Landscape*, eds. Joel Martin and Mark A. Nicholas (Chapel Hill: University of North Carolina Press, 2010), 201.

30 See Berkhofer, *Salvation*, 176; and Margaret Connell Szasz, *Indian Education in the American Colonies, 1607–1783* (Albuquerque: University of New Mexico Press, 1988).

31 Civilization Fund Act (1819), *U.S. Statutes at Large*, 3:516–17. See also Berkhofer, *White Man's Indian*, 149.

32 See Ronald N. Satz, *American Indian Policy in the Jacksonian Era* (Norman: University of Oklahoma Press, 1975), 253.

33 William H. Armstrong, *Warrior in Two Camps: Ely S. Parker, Union General, and Seneca Chief* (New York:

Syracuse University Press, 1978), 21. See also Satz, *Indian Policy*, 247; and Hauptman, *Tonawanda*, chapter 3.

34 See Alyssa Mt. Pleasant, "After the Whirlwind: Maintaining a Haudenosaunee Place at Buffalo Creek, 1780–1825" (PhD diss., Cornell University, 2007), 174.

35 Buffalo Creek Seneca chiefs to President Martin Van Buren, October 2, 1837, M234/583, NARA.

36 "Chiefs and Sachems of the Six Nations of Indians residing in the State of New York" to President Martin Van Buren, February 10, 1838, M234/583, NARA. See also Berkhofer, *Salvation*, 176.

37 Buffalo Creek Seneca chiefs to President Martin Van Buren, October 2, 1837, M234/583, NARA.

38 Ibid.

39 Tonawanda chiefs (incl. John Blacksmith) to President John Tyler, July 12, 1843, M234/585, NARA. See also Elisabeth Tooker, "The League of the Iroquois: Its History, Politics, and Ritual," in *Handbook of North American Indians. Volume 15: Northeast*, ed. Bruce G. Trigger (Washington, D.C.: Smithsonian Institution, 1978), 426; and Elisabeth Tooker, "Women in Iroquois Society," in *Extending the Rafters*, eds. Michael K. Foster, Jack Campisi, and Marianne Mithun (Albany: State University of New York Press, 1984), 112. For a discussion of those messages written by Senecas supporting removal, see Claudia B. Haake, "'In the Same Predicament as Heretofore': Pro-Removal Arguments in Iroquois Letters in the 1830s and 1840s," *Ethnohistory* 61, no. 1 (2014): 57–78.

40 Buffalo Creek Seneca chiefs to President Martin Van Buren, October 2, 1837, M234/583, NARA. Israel Jimeson, Seneca White, and others of Cattaraugus to Robert H. Shankland, subagent for the New York Indians, September 29, 1848, M234/587, NARA.

41 See Deborah A. Rosen, *American Indians and State Law: Sovereignty, Race, and Citizenship* (Lincoln: University of Nebraska Press, 2007), 207. See also Hauptman, *Conspiracy*.

42 John Blacksmith, Jemmy Johnson, and others of Tonawanda to Commissioner of Indian Affairs Orlando Brown, June 23, 1849, M234/588, NARA.

43 None mentioned formerly important concepts like the tree of peace, the burying of the axe, fire as a symbol of civil government, the path as one of communication, or the theme of "one heart."

44 Wampum was used from seventeenth to eighteenth century as currency in trade and for negotiations. See for instance Fenton, *Great Law*, 7.

45 William N. Fenton, "Leadership in the Northeastern Woodlands of America," *American Indian Quarterly*, The History of American Indian Leadership, vol. 10, no. 1 (Winter 1986): 25.

46 Penny van Toorn, *Writing Never Arrives Naked: Early Aboriginal Cultures of Writing in Australia* (Canberra, Australia: Aboriginal Studies Press, 2006), 21. See also Brooks, *Common Pot*.

47 See Fenton, *Great Law*, 234.

48 Mary A. Druke, "Iroquois Treaties: Common Forms, Varying Interpretations," in *The History and Culture of Iroquois Diplomacy: An Interdisciplinary Guide to the Treaties of the Six Nations and Their League*, eds. Francis Jennings, William N. Fenton, Mary A. Druke, and David R. Miller (Syracuse: Syracuse University Press, 1985), 88; and Fenton, *Great Law*, 559.

49 See William N. Fenton, "Structure, Continuity, and Change in the Process of Iroquois Treaty Making," in *History and Culture of Iroquois Diplomacy*, 26. For another dimension, see also Tony Ballantyne, "Talking, Listening, Writing, Reading: Communication and Colonialism" (The Allan Martin Lecture 2009, The Australian National University), 11.

50 See Round, *Removable Type*, 106; and Brooks, *Common Pot*, xxii.

51 See Herman J. Viola, *Diplomats in Buckskins: A History of Indian Delegations in Washington City* (Bluffton, S.C.: Rivilo Books, 1995), 155.

52 See Denson, *Demanding*, 2004.

53 Brooks, *Common Pot*, 241.

54 Ibid., 225.

55 See James H. Merrell, *Into the American Woods: Negotiators on the Pennsylvania Frontier* (New York: Norton, 1999), 195–97.

56 See Fenton, *Great Law*, 638; and Merrell, *Into the American Woods*, 193 and 197. See also Daniel K. Richter, "The States, the United States and the Canandaigua Treaty," in *Treaty of Canandaigua 1794: 200 Years of Treaty Relations between the Iroquois Confederacy and the United States*, eds. G. Peter Jemison and Anna M. Schein (Santa Fe, N. Mex.: Clear Light, 2000), 76.

57 See Daniel K. Richter, *Facing East from Indian Country: A Native History of Early America* (Cambridge, Mass.: Harvard University Press, 2001), 137.

58 See Brooks, *Common Pot*, 241.

59 Matthew Dennis, "Sorcery and Sovereignty: Senecas, Citizens, and the Contest for Power and Authority on the Frontiers of the Early American Republic," in *New World Orders: Violence, Sanction, and Authority in the Colonial Americas*, eds. John Smolenski and Thomas J. Humphrey (Philadelphia: University of Pennsylvania Press, 2005), 189.

60 Laurence M. Hauptman, *The Iroquois and the New Deal* (Syracuse, N.Y.: Syracuse University Press, 1981), 3.

61 Buffalo Creek Seneca chiefs to President Martin Van Buren, October 2, 1837, M234/583, NARA.

62 William Patterson, Meeting on November 3 with Allegany chiefs, in William Devereux to Commissioner of Indian Affairs Hartley Crawford, no date (1840), M234/584, NARA.

63 John Blacksmith, Jemmy Johnson, and others of Tonawanda to Commissioner of Indian Affairs Orlando Brown, June 23, 1849, M234/587, NARA. See also Hauptman, *Tonawanda*, 31, 39, and 66.

64 Zachariah Jimeson, President, to Secretary of the Interior Alexander H. H. Stuart ("Stewart"), November 23, 1850, M234/587, NARA; Israel Jimeson and others to unnamed president, December 12, 1853, M234/588, NARA.

65 See Maureen Konkle, *Writing Indian Nations: Native Intellectuals and the Politics of Historiography, 1827–1863* (Chapel Hill: University of North Carolina Press, 2004), 231.

66 Shoemaker, *Strange Likeness*, 71.

67 See Hauptman, *Tonawanda*, xxii, 61, 64, 73, 76.

68 S. W. MacLane, president of Seneca Nation, to Secretary of the Interior Thomas Ewing, November 7, 1849, M234/587, NARA.

69 Joshua Turkey and others to Commissioner of Indian Affairs George W. Manypenny, February 19, 1855, M234/588, NARA. See also Michael K. Foster, *From the Earth to Beyond the Sky: An Ethno-*

graphic Approach to Four Longhouse Iroquois Speech Events (Ottawa, Ont.: National Museum of Canada, 1974), 206.

70 See Thomas S. Abler, ed., *Chainbreaker: The Revolutionary War Memoirs of Governor Blacksnake as Told to Benjamin Williams* (Lincoln: University of Nebraska Press, 1989), 11. For a different opinion, see Martinez, *Tradition*, xii.

71 See Fenton, *Great Law*, 29.

72 Fenton, "Structure, Continuity, and Change," 21. This number refers to the more substantial letters sent, excluding for instance very short messages such as ones inquiring about delayed annuities.

73 See, for instance, Timothy J. Shannon, *Iroquois Diplomacy on the Early American Frontier* (New York: Penguin, 2008); Gail D. MacLeitch, *Imperial Entanglements: Iroquois Change and Persistence on the Frontiers of Empire* (Philadelphia: University of Pennsylvania Press, 2011); Fenton, *Great Law*; and Richard White, *The Middle Ground: Indians, Empires, and Republics in the Great Lakes Region, 1650–1815* (Cambridge, Mass.: Cambridge University Press, 1991).

74 For colonial era examples, see Viola, *Diplomats in Buckskins*, 20. Several communications on file at the Indian Office also show examples of such forms of address used when writing or talking to Indians.

75 Buffalo Creek chiefs and headmen to Secretary of War Lewis Cass, October 4, 1835, M234/583, NARA. See also Seneca chiefs to President Martin Van Buren, January 7, 1839, M234/583, NARA; Little Johnson, Captain John Pollard, and others from Buffalo Creek to President Martin Van Buren, November 25, 1840, M234/584, NARA; Elijah Schenandoah and others to President Millard Fillmore, March 30, 1852, M234/588, NARA. Moses Schuyler, head chief, and Abraham Schuyler, chief, at Onondaga Castle, to President Martin Van Buren, August 17, 1837, M234/583, NARA. See also "Chiefs and Sachems of the Six Nations of Indians residing in the State of New York" to President Martin Van Buren, February 10, 1838, M234/583, NARA.

76 John Blacksmith and others to President James K. Polk, May 7, 1846, M234/586; Seneca chiefs to President James K. Polk, January 25, 1849, M234/587, NARA; Andrew Snow and others to President Millard Fillmore, April 21, 1852, M234/588, NARA.

77 Seneca chiefs to President James K. Polk, January 25, 1849, M234/587, NARA.

78 Onondaga chiefs to "Great Father," August 11, 1837, M234/583, NARA; James Cusick and others to President Martin Van Buren, September 4, 1845, M234/586, NARA.

79 Captain Strong, Little Johnson, White Seneca, and others of Buffalo Creek to President John Tyler, June 19, 1840, M234/584, NARA.

80 Governor Blacksnake and others to President William Henry Harrison, March 4, 1841, M234/584, NARA. Tonawanda chiefs to President John Tyler, January 9, 1843, M234/585, NARA.

81 Tonawanda chiefs to President John Tyler, January 9, 1843, M234/585, NARA.

82 Chiefs of Tonawanda and Buffalo reservations to President John Tyler, February 1, 1843, M234/585, NARA.

83 Buffalo Creek chief and warriors to President John Tyler, May 23, 1844, M234/585, NARA.

84 Ibid.

85 Petition from Little Johnson, Captain Strong, and others, March 28, 1840, M234/584, NARA. See also William Parker and others to President Franklin Pierce, October 7, 1856, M234/588, NARA. For an analysis of how the Iroquois at times rejected this status, see Claudia B. Haake, "Iroquois Use of Customary Haudenosaunee and United States Law in Opposing Removal," *American Indian Culture and Research Journal* 36, no. 4 (2012): 29–56.

86 See also Konstantin Dierks, *In My Power: Letter Writing and Communications in Early America* (Philadelphia: University of Pennsylvania Press, 2009).

87 Tonawanda chiefs, including John Blacksmith, to President John Tyler, July 12, 1843, M234/585, NARA.

88 Richard White, "The Fictions of Patriarchy: Indians and Whites in the Early Republic," in *Native Americans and the Early Republic*, eds. Frederick E. Hoxie, Ronald Hoffman, and Peter J. Albert (Charlotteville, Va.: United States Capitol Historical Society, 1999), 64–84. See also White, *Middle Ground*, 268; and Jane T. Merritt, *At the Crossroads: Indians and Empires on a Mid-Atlantic Frontier, 1700–1763* (Chapel Hill: University of North Carolina Press, 2003), 214–215. For an insightful discussion of the middle ground, see Philip J. Deloria, "What Is the Middle Ground, Anyway?," *William and Mary Quarterly* 63 (January 2006): 15–22.

89 See, for instance, Daniel K. Richter, "Onas, the Long Knife: Pennsylvanians and Indians, 1783–1794," in *Native Americans and the Early Republic*, 124. See also Fenton, *Great Law*, 320, 526.

90 See Richter, *Facing East*, 138. There were, however, distinctions between older and younger brothers.

91 Fenton, *Great Law*, 254, 307.

92 Richter, "Onas," 155.

93 Richter, *Facing East*, 226.

94 Peter Doxtater and others to Charles E. Mix, July 17, 1851, M234/587, NARA. See also Silversmith at Buffalo Creek Reservation to unnamed Secretary of War, December 15, 1843, M234/585, NARA.

95 Tonawanda chiefs to Secretary of War James B. Price [judging by the date this should be James M. Porter], October 24, 1843, M234/585, NARA.

96 In spite of having multiple signatories and also using "we," the letter also uses "I," indicating that it originated as a compromise and through the input of several people.

97 Tonawanda chiefs to Secretary of War J. M. Porter, December 30, 1843, M234/585, NARA.

98 John Blacksmith and James Johnson at Batavia to Secretary of War William Wilkins, August 20, 1844, M234/585, NARA.

99 Ibid.

100 Tonawanda chiefs to Secretary of War John C. Spencer, June 5, 1843, M234/585, NARA.

101 Buffalo Creek chiefs to President John Tyler, March 29, 1844, M234/585, NARA. For other "combination" letters, see Tonawanda chiefs to Judge Love, October 17, 1843, M234/585, NARA; and James Cusick to Secretary of War William L. Marcy, April 3, 1847, M234/586, NARA.

102 See, for instance, William Mountpleasant and others to Griffith M. Cooper, August 4, 1841, M234/584, NARA; Israel Jemison and Seneca

White to Philip E. Thomas, undated, summer 1848, M234/587, NARA.

103   See Haake, "Iroquois Use of Customary and United States Law" and "In the Same Predicament as Heretofore."

104   See Connell Szasz, *Indian Education*, chapter 10, on Indian teachers.

105   See Laura J. Murray, *To Do Good to My Indian Brethren: The Writings of Joseph Johnson, 1751–1776* (Amherst: University of Massachusetts Press, 1998), 11.

106   See Lucille M. Schultz, "Letter-Writing Instruction in Nineteenth-Century Schools in the United States," in *Letter Writing as a Social Practice*, eds. David Barton and Nigel Hall (Philadelphia, Pa.: John Benjamins Publishing, 1999), 115; and Dierks, *In My Power.*

107   See Hauptman, *Tonawanda*, chapter 6; and C. Joseph Genetin-Pilawa, *Crooked Paths to Allotment: The Fight over Federal Indian Policy after the Civil War* (Chapel Hill: University of North Carolina Press, 2012).

108   See Colin G. Calloway, *The Indian History of an American Institution: Native Americans and Dartmouth* (Hanover, N.H., and London: University Press of New England, 2010); and H. A. Vernon, "Maris Bryant Pierce," in *Indian Lives: Essays on Nineteenth- and Twentieth-Century Native American Leaders*, eds. L. G. Moses and Raymond Wilson (Albuquerque: University of New Mexico Press, 1990).

109   See David Barton and Nigel Hall, "Introduction," in *Letter Writing as a Social Practice*, 3.

110   See Round, *Removable Type*, 140.

111   S. W. MacLane, President of Seneca Nation, to Secretary of the Interior Thomas Ewing, November 7, 1849, M234/587, NARA.

112   For speeches, see Michael K. Foster, "When Words Become Deeds: An Analysis of Three Iroquois Longhouse Speech Events," in *Explorations in the Ethnography of Speaking*, eds. Richard Bauman and Joel Sherzer (Cambridge, Mass.: Cambridge University Press, 1989); Harry Robie, "Red Jacket's Reply: Problems in the Verification of a Native American Speech Text," *New York Folklore* 12, nos. 3–4 (1986); and Foster, *From the Earth*, 206.

113   See Fenton, *Great Law*, 30.

114   Seneca chiefs to President James K. Polk, January 25, 1849, M234/587, NARA.

115   See Foster, *From the Earth*, 172; and Michael K. Foster, "One Who Spoke First at Iroquois-White Councils: An Exercise in the Method of Upstreaming," in *Extending the Rafters: Interdisciplinary Approaches to Iroquoian Studies*, eds. Michael K. Foster, Jack Campisi, and Marianne Mithun (Albany: State University of New York Press, 1984), 184.

116   Committee of Safety Seneca Nation of Indians to President Millard Fillmore, December 20, 1851, M234/588, NARA.

117   Ibid.

118   Israel Jimeson and others to unnamed president, December 12, 1853, M234/588, NARA.

119   See Committee from Cold Spring to President William Henry Harrison, March 4, 1841, HR27A-G8.1, NARA.

120   See especially Tooker, "Women in Iroquois Society," 113; Tooker, "The League," 422; and Fenton, *Great Law*, 509.

121   See Anthony F. C. Wallace, *The Death and Rebirth of the Seneca* (New York: Knopf, 1970), 202. See also Hauptman, *Tonawanda*, 72.

122 While in the first edition of Abler's *Chainbreaker*, the author gives 1753 as Blacksnake's date of birth, the second edition speculates that he may not have been born until ten years later. However, this does not affect my argument. Abler, *Chainbreaker*, 221.

123 See Abler, *Chainbreaker*, 15.

124 Haake, "Iroquois Use of Customary and United States Law."

125 See Lisa Ford, *Settler Sovereignty: Jurisdiction and Indigenous People in America and Australia, 1788–1836* (Cambridge, Mass.: Harvard University Press, 2010), 3.

126 The subsequent *Cherokee Nation* and *Worcester* decisions by Chief Justice Marshall implicitly rejected New York's 1822 legislation as unconstitutional but in practice this mattered little. See Matthew Dennis, *Seneca Possessed: Indians, Witchcraft, and Power in the Early American Republic* (Philadelphia: University of Pennsylvania Press, 2010), 24.

127 Shoemaker, *A Strange Likeness*, 8.

128 See Inga Clendinnen, "Reading Mr Robinson," *Australian Book Review* (May 1995): 39.

129 Teuton, *Deep Waters*, 23. See also Drew Lopenzina, *Red Ink: Native Americans Picking up the Pen in the Colonial Period* (Albany: State University of New York Press, 2012), 13.

130 Robert Warrior, *The People and the Word: Reading Native Nonfiction* (Minneapolis: University of Minnesota Press, 2005), xiii.

"No General Use Can Ever Be Made of the Wrecks of My Loss"

A Reconsidered History of the Indian Vocabularies Collected on the Lewis and Clark Expedition

Megan Snyder-Camp

Hoping that comparative linguistics would show that Native languages descended from European or Asian roots, Thomas Jefferson collected dozens of standardized Native language word lists, or Indian vocabularies. He asked Lewis and Clark to expand his database during their 1804 to 1806 journey, and they did so, collecting 280-word keys to at least twenty-three Indian languages, many from tribes west of the Mississippi whose words had never before been written down. None of these vocabularies were ever published. In 1809, three years after the Lewis and Clark expedition, a thief threw Indian vocabularies belonging to Jefferson overboard into the James River. American history scholars have consistently, and mistakenly, claimed that the Indian vocabularies collected by Lewis and Clark were among the Indian vocabularies destroyed during this theft.

New findings reopen what has previously been described as a simple story of unfortunate loss. From previously unpublished handwritten court records, I have identified the man convicted of stealing Jefferson's Indian vocabularies and the details of his arrest, conviction, and sentencing. From Jefferson's late correspondence and from the inventory taken at the site of Lewis's death three months after the trial, I offer clear evidence that Lewis and Clark's Indian vocabularies were not among those stolen. These new findings both alter the historical narrative and also offer a narrowed field to any Native scholars interested in pursuing and reclaiming these "lost" vocabularies.

Hoping to prove that Native languages descended from European or Asian roots, Thomas Jefferson began collecting Indian vocabularies in 1791, and over the next thirty years he amassed about sixty Indian vocabularies. Jefferson created his own 280-word printed card-stock template of common English words. It is an oversize sheet that folds into quadrants for travel, with constellations of related words beginning with *fire* and ending with *no*. There is room next to each English word for its Native equivalent, but no room on the page for any context: no space for observations of the people or the community, though at times a field collector might scrawl a few notes in the margin. No room for grammar, either.

When Jefferson sent Meriwether Lewis and William Clark on their 1804 to 1806 journey across the United States, one of the tasks the explorers were assigned was to collect Indian vocabularies—written lists of Native equivalents to common English words—during interactions with as many of the Indian communities they met along their route as possible.[1] Jefferson lamented that so many Native tribes had disappeared "without our having previously collected and deposited in the records of literature the general rudiments at least of the languages they spoke."[2]

When Jefferson began to compare Indian vocabularies, it was quickly obvious that not only was his tongue not the father of these languages, but that Native languages showed a diversity and complexity that indicated Native cultures had existed here for a very long time, diverging and merging by turn as cultures do over tens of thousands of years.[3] The extended history indicated by this diversity was particularly observable in the grammars of the languages, which built their sentences so very differently than European and Asian models, and showed several distinct Native language families as well. Grammar is thought, is logic, is worldview. Each language builds a particular city map in the brains of those who speak it. Jefferson, and most other early American amateur linguists during the early years of interaction, quickly found themselves in cities they could not navigate. Cities that were not laid out by European or Asian planners, but were older and more complex.

During the early years of European contact, Native languages showed what the land did not. The long history indicated by the complex city maps of these languages stood in contrast to the ravaged appearance of Native cities and towns themselves, which had been under attack for the preceding three decades as successive epidemics of influenza and smallpox swept back and forth across the land.[4] Perceiving the Natives they met as powerless, impoverished, transient—members of a dying race—whose towns were now ruins and abandoned, their lands empty and available, the explorers found it in their own best interest to minimize contrary indications of a long and prosperous Native history, indications that included the complex languages they heard as they passed through, spoken by the survivors of these epidemics, who were now their guides.

The vast majority of these Indian vocabularies were never published. The period of intense Euro-American interest in Native languages, a period during which many Native language vocabularies were collected by amateur fieldworkers hoping to capture the last echoes of a disappearing civilization, ended with a scholarly silence that has continued. As the young U.S. government began to create the reservation system, and other forms of systemically removing Native people from their land, U.S. engagement with Native language and culture sharply waned. One of the ways in which the explorers, and the generations of white American scholars in their wake, have hampered the continuing work of Native language preservation is by abandoning these early, vital, irreplaceable records without publishing them or sharing them with contemporary Native linguists.

I am a white American poet. My second book of poems, *Wintering* (forthcoming in 2016 from Tupelo Press), is engaged with the November of Lewis and Clark's arrival at the Pacific Ocean. The explorers were miserable that winter, and built a fort to protect themselves. The password the men whispered to each other at the gate to their fort was *No Chinook.*[5] That winter, the men collected Indian vocabularies, as they did throughout the expedition, for a total of at least twenty-three. In my study, I read dozens of scholarly versions of the explorers' November, each version slightly different from the last. I became curious about what happened to all of the Indian vocabularies they collected, and as I began to search for that chapter of the story, I was puzzled to find that all scholarly accounts of the vocabularies' fate seem to use the same boilerplate text: after the expedition, the vocabularies were sadly lost. If the text expands beyond that, it is to say that after the expedition, the vocabularies were sadly lost when a thief stole them from a trunk belonging to Thomas Jefferson. The thief was tricked by the heaviness of the trunk into thinking that the trunk contained gold or other items of value. On opening the trunk and discovering the paper vocabularies, the frustrated thief flung them into the James River, where they were ruined beyond repair. After encountering nearly identical phrasing in dozens of otherwise nuanced and engaging texts,[6] I wondered if there were more to this chapter of the story. I began by trying to find out the thief's name.

To my surprise, significant and until-now unpublished details of this story rose smoothly to the surface. What I found differs starkly from the narrative most Lewis and Clark historians seem to agree on.[7] Using handwritten court records brittle-folded in an envelope at the Library of Virginia, Jefferson's post-presidency correspondence at Monticello, and the Sappho-like vocabulary fragments at the American Philosophical Society, among other carefully cataloged, but empty, folders, I began to piece together a fuller, more complex narrative of the fate of the Indian vocabularies collected during the Lewis and Clark expedition.

During the two-year expedition, Lewis recorded at least twenty-three Indian vocabularies, about a dozen of which were from tribes located west of the Mississippi, whose languages had never been recorded in written form before. He sent two (the Iowa and the Sioux) back with Captain Amos Stoddard, and another nine back from Saint Louis in the fall of 1806. He brought the remaining ten to twelve vocabularies back to Jefferson in person at the end of the journey. After showing the vocabularies to Jefferson, and likely allowing them to be copied, Lewis asked Jefferson for permission to keep his originals so that he might publish those vocabularies along with his journals and scientific findings from the expedition. In his 1807 prospectus for the material he planned to publish, Lewis stated that the second volume of the account "will contain a comparative view of twenty three vocabularies of distinct Indian languages, procured by Captains Lewis and Clark on the voyage."[8]

This, along with an 1829 letter from Jefferson, shows that the Indian vocabularies Lewis collected were not among Jefferson's stolen Indian vocabulary collection. By the time the Corps of Discovery set out, Jefferson had twenty-two Indian vocabularies, taken from tribes east of the Mississippi. With the help of a variety of amateur collectors, over the course of thirty years that collection grew to thirty or forty Indian vocabularies from tribes east of the Mississippi. These originals, as well as any copies Jefferson may have received in his frequent correspondence with other linguists, were likely what was destroyed during the riverboat theft.

While president, Jefferson often traveled between the White House and the house he was building at Monticello in the Virginia hills. He often shipped dozens of trunks of his possessions ahead of him. These trunks traveled by boat from the White House down the Potomac River to the Chesapeake Bay and up the James River to Richmond, and then were transferred to smaller boats for the last leg of their journey up one of the two private canals on Jefferson's Monticello estate.

Loss was not uncommon. On June 4, 1807, Jefferson wrote to Lewis regarding the fate of one of his animal artifacts after one of these trips: "The horns, which I could not take on with me, were packed into one of 25 boxes, barrels, &c. which I sent round by water. The vessel was stranded, and everything lost which water could injure."[9] In his June 27 reply, Lewis writes, "I sincerely regret the loss you sustained in the articles you shiped for Richmond; it seems peculiarly unfortunate that those at least, which had passed the continent of America and after their exposure to so many casualties and wrisks should have met such destiny in their passage through a small portion only of the Chesapeak."[10] Earlier that month, Lewis had published the prospectus for his account of the 1804 to 1806 expedition, and surely the safety of his Indian vocabularies was on his mind.

The second loss—the one that has been erroneously linked to the Indian vocabularies Lewis collected—took place in May of 1809 as Jefferson ended his presidential term and left the capital for the last time. Jefferson's boat, loaded with twenty-nine trunks, waited overnight in Richmond, Virginia, in the James River Canal basin, anchored near Pickets Lumber Yard, watched over by an unnamed boatman. In the early morning hours, one of the trunks was stolen. Jefferson hadn't made an inventory of the trunks' contents, but over the next few weeks he created, and added to, a list of what was missing. On June 16, his cousin George placed an ad in the Richmond *Enquirer* for the trunk, which "contained principally writing paper of various qualities, but also some other articles of stationary, a pocket telescope with a brass case, a Dynamometer in steel and brass, or instrument for measuring the exertions of draught animals, a collection of vocabularies of the Indian languages, & some other articles not particularly noted in the memorandum taken."[11]

From a July 1809 letter to George Jefferson from Samuel J. Harrison,[12] a local tobacco merchant and Lynchburg alderman, it appears that Jefferson asked Harrison to carry out the search for a thief. Harrison accused Ned, "a Noted Villain," and a slave owned by the recently deceased James B. Couch of Buckingham County, of the theft. According to Harrison, "he Threw it, with the Balance of the articles overboard, just below Britains Landing, nearly opposite westham."[13] On July 25, 1809, in Richmond, Virginia, a court of Oyer and Terminer was convened to hear the case.[14] Oyer and Terminer courts are a particular style of closed courts, used in slave trials and in the Salem witch trials.[15] Thomas Jefferson was not present at the trial, which lasted less than a day.

Here is my transcription of the sole piece of evidence filed, a letter handwritten by Richmond mayor John Lynch Jr.:

Whereas H. Parrington of the corporation aforesaid and
hath given information, this day upon oath, to me John
Lynch Jr. mayor of said corporation, that he is advised
by George Jefferson of the City of Richmond, that on or
about the day of last past at or near the City of Richmond,
there was feloniously taken, stolen, and carried away
from on Board a Certain Batteau, the property of [space
left blank] then [2 words illegible] the city of Richmond,
the Canal locks, a certain trunk, the property of Thomas
Jefferson Esquire [. . .] was taken, stolen, & carried away
by Ned, a Negro man slave, the property of the Estate of
James B. Couch, dec'd, late of the County of Buckingham,

[illegible] are therefore in the name of the Commonwealth [illegible] to apprehend the slave Ned, & to bring him before me, to answer the premises & further to be dealt with according to law—Given and in my hand this 13th day of July 1809.

George Jefferson told H. Parrington, who swore to John Lynch Jr. that Ned was the thief. Lynch found Ned "guilty of felony and doth order that he be burnt in the left hand and receive thirty nine lashes on his bare back at the public whipping post."[16]

It is unclear whether Lewis, living in Louisiana at the time, heard about this incident in which Jefferson's Indian vocabularies were destroyed. But that summer, Lewis, who had still not published his journals from the expedition, or any of his Indian vocabularies, became increasingly paranoid about the risk of his papers falling into the wrong hands. In September 1809, Lewis left for a trip to Washington, D.C., in hopes of resolving some of his ongoing personal financial problems, and then to Philadelphia to deliver the expedition-related papers to the publisher who had agreed to bring out the work. He had initially planned to travel by water but then decided the water route was too dangerous, and so traveled through the Chickasaw Nation by land, stating in a letter to President James Madison dated September 16, 1809, "My apprehension from the heat of the lower country and my fear of the original papers relative to my voyage falling into the hands of the British has induced me to change my rout and proceed by land through the state of Tennisee to the City of washington."[17]

Waiting in Philadelphia was Benjamin Smith Barton, a self-taught linguist and pediatrician, who has been portrayed as both Jefferson's collaborator and a competitor, who also helped to train Lewis in the practice of collecting Indian vocabularies. He wrote to Jefferson on September 14, 1809, with the news that he was about to publish a book on American Indian languages, stating, "I am extremely anxious to possess specimens—no matter how small,—of the languages which Mr. Lewis met with beyond the Mississippi. I will think myself much gratified, and honoured, if you will transmit to me, as early as your convenience may suit, such specimens."[18] Where Jefferson's handwriting is tiny, precise, and upright, Barton's is loose, scrawled, barreling forward.

Jefferson, in his September 21 reply, described the thirty years he had dedicated to amassing a comprehensive collection of about fifty Indian vocabularies,[19] a period during which he notes that his "opportunities were probably better than will ever occur again to any person having the same desire." By the time of this 1809 incident, he had not, however, published or even fully studied the vocabularies he possessed, and so when the bulk of his collection was dropped into the river that day, any record was lost. As Jefferson notes in his letter to Barton,

Some leaves floated ashore & were found in the mud; but
these were very few, & so defaced by the mud & water that
no general use can ever be made of them. On the reciept
of your letter I turned to them, & was very happy to find
that the only morsel of an original vocabulary among them
was Capt Lewis's of the Pani language of which you say
you have not one word. I therefore inclose it to you, as it is,
& a little fragment of some other, which I see is in his handwriting, but no indication remains on it of what language
it is. [. . .] altho I believe no general use can ever be made of
the wrecks of my loss, yet I will ask the return of the Pani
vocabulary when you are done with it. perhaps I may make
another attempt to collect, altho' I am too old to expect to
make much progress in it. [. . .][20]

Early in the morning of October 11, 1809, having only made it
as far as Nashville, Lewis shot himself. In the Memorandum of Lewis'
Personal Effects,[21] dated November 23, "one do. vocabulary" is listed,
with the note that it was forwarded on, with all other items relating to
the expedition, to William Clark. Clark's responsibility at that point
was to find someone to help write the narrative of the journey, and to
prepare the journals for publication. Clark took the expedition-related
papers to Philadelphia, and Nicholas Biddle (who published the first
account of the expedition, in 1814) delivered the Indian vocabularies
to Barton. In 1810, Barton wrote to Jefferson, "In regard to Mr. Lewis's
papers, I assure you, and I beg you, Sir, to assure his friends, that they
will be taken good care of; that it is my sincere wish to turn them, as
much as I can, to his honour & reputation; and that they shall ultimately
be deposited, in good order, in the hands of General Clark, or those of
Mr. Conrad, the publisher. During the Governor's [Lewis's] last visit to
Philadelphia, there was some difference between him and me."[22]

Barton died in 1815. He did not publish any of Lewis's vocabularies
during his lifetime. In a letter dated April 26, 1816, to José Corrèa da
Serra (who would soon become Spanish minister to the United States),
Jefferson wrote of Lewis's Indian vocabularies,

I had myself made a collection of about 40. vocabularies
of the Indians on this side of the Missisipi, and Capt. Lewis
was instructed to take those of every tribe beyond, which
he possibly could: the intention was to publish the whole,
and leave the world to search for affinities between these
and the languages of Europe and Asia. He was furnished
with a number of printed vocabularies of the same words
and form I had used, with blank spaces for the Indian words.
He was very attentive to this instruction, never missing an

opportunity of taking a vocabulary. After his return, he asked me if I should have any objection to the printing his separately, as mine was not yet arranged as I intended. I assured him I had no objection; and I am certain he contemplated their publication. But whether he had put the papers out of his own hand or not, I do not know. I imagine he had not: and it is probable that Doctr. Barton, who was particularly curious on this subject, and published on it occasionally, would willingly receive and take care of these papers after Capt. Lewis's death, and that they are now among his papers.[23]

In 1817, Jefferson offered the remains of his Indian vocabularies to the American Philosophical Society, with the acknowledgment that the ones Lewis collected had not yet been returned by Barton's estate.[24] In an April 6, 1818, letter to American Philosophical Society Historical Committee Chair William Tilghman, Biddle recalls delivering the Indian vocabularies to Barton after Lewis's death:

My recollection is not as accurate as it would have been had they fallen more immediately under my examination. My impression however is that [. . .] the papers were Indian vocabularies, collected during the journey. They formed, I think, a bundle of loose sheets each sheet containing a printed vocabulary in English with the corresponding Indian name in manuscript. [. . .] In the preface to the printed travels which, being published in Phila. whilst Dr. Barton was there, must be presumed to have been correct it is stated that "[. . .] the alphabets of the Indian languages are in the hands of Professor Barton, and will it is understood, shortly appear." This was in 1814. I have mentioned these particulars so minutely because their description may perhaps enable some members of the Committee to recognize the vocabularies, which I incline to think were the only things delivered to me by Dr. Barton not included in the volumes now deposited.[25]

Why, in the seventeen years after he lost his East Coast Indian vocabularies, didn't Jefferson make a stronger effort to retrieve Lewis's vocabularies from the successions of linguists and publishers who held them? Perhaps he had already gotten from the vocabularies what he wanted: an answer to the question of whether the tribal languages bore European or Asian roots.[26] They did not, and so, in Jefferson's mind, they might not have warranted his continued study. On February 20,

1825, just eighteen months before his death, Jefferson wrote to the linguist John Pickering of the vast differences in the grammars of Native and European languages, stating, "I believe we shall find it impossible to translate our language into any of the Indian, or any of theirs into ours."[27] I believe that Jefferson found the theft to be a convenient opportunity to wash his hands of a field of study he had grown disinterested in. Successive scholars have continued to conflate the riverboat theft with the loss of Lewis's Indian vocabularies, obscuring the path for any linguists who might find use in recovering these documents. Considering how easily I, a non-scholar, was able to locate significant "new" findings, I would be truly surprised if there is not more to be found, perhaps including the vocabularies themselves, information that belongs to contemporary Native linguists.

Some of Barton's papers, along with Jefferson's, are held at the American Philosophical Society.[28] Among them are Indian vocabularies, most still unpublished, as well as the carefully archived muddy remnants of the ones fished from the James River. Searching every file, I could find no trace of the Indian vocabularies Lewis painstakingly collected. That doesn't mean they can't be found. "You can't say that Lewis's vocabularies are lost," the archivist at the American Philosophical Society reminded me at the end of my three-day search. "It's only that you did not find them."

These distinctive vocabularies, on oversize card stock, would be unlikely to have ever been mistaken for scrap. A deeper search among Barton's papers, or a search among the papers of other amateur linguists with whom Barton exchanged language samples in search of these particular vocabularies, has not yet been undertaken.

As a white poet whose archival work over the past five years has ushered me into many small, closed rooms of "findings" stored out of sight in museum attics or in library special collections, I feel a responsibility to speak out against the combination of scholarly hoarding and neglect I have encountered, and to try not to perpetuate the mentality of early American settlers myself. It is not my place to continue the search for these vocabularies: they are not mine to find. And whether or not these particular Indian vocabularies are ever located, is my hope that this part of the story might be of use to Native scholars and linguists, and that a correction of the historical account will encourage Lewis and Clark scholars to tackle the sticky questions raised here, rather than portray this chapter as closed.

AUTHOR BIOGRAPHY

Megan Snyder-Camp is the author of *The Forest of Sure Things: Poems* (2010) and *Wintering* (forthcoming).

Some of the research for this work was supported by an Individual Artist grant from Washington State's 4Culture Foundation.

1   Robert J. Miller, *Native America, Discovered and Conquered: Thomas Jefferson, Lewis and Clark, and Manifest Destiny* (Westport, Conn.: Prager, 2006), 103–4.

2   Thomas Jefferson, *Notes on the State of Virginia* (London: John Stockdale, 1787), 164.

3   Andrew H. Fisher, *Shadow Tribe: The Making of Columbia River Indian Identity* (Seattle: University of Washington Press, 2010).

4   Colin G. Calloway, *One Vast Winter Count: The Native American West before Lewis and Clark* (Lincoln: University of Nebraska Press, 2006).

5   Donald Jackson, ed., *Letters of the Lewis and Clark Expedition: With Related Documents 1783–1854* (Champaign: University of Illinois Press, 1962). From the Nicholas Biddle Notes [ca. April 1810]: a note on November 15, 1805, written by Biddle during a conversation with William Clark, 541.

6   Charles Boewe, "George Shannon and C. S. Rafinesque," in *Lewis and Clark: Legacies, Memories, and New Perspectives*, eds. Kris Fresonke and Mark Spence (Berkeley: University of California Press, 2004), 150–51. "Since the vocabularies collected by Lewis apparently were lost when Jefferson's possessions were rifled on the James River while being shipped to Monticello, even the few words recalled by Shannon now add another heirloom to the memorabilia of the Corps of Discovery. They add nothing, of course, to present-day understanding of Indian languages [. . .]." Carolyn Gilman, *Lewis and Clark: Across the Divide* (Washington, D.C.: Smithsonian Books, 2003), 298–99.

    "Even more tragic was the fate of the linguistic evidence so laboriously collected by Lewis. En route to Monticello from Washington, D.C., one of Jefferson's trunks containing the word lists was stolen, and its contents were thrown in the river. When he heard of their destruction, Lewis remarked painfully on the irony that they 'had passed the continent of America and after their exposure to so many wrisks and casualties [they] should have met such destiny in their passage through a small portion only of the Chesapeak.'" (Note: this letter from Lewis actually refers to a prior instance of loss of Native artifacts, not the vocabularies, as I discuss later in this paper.) James P. Ronda, *Lewis and Clark among the Indians* (Lincoln: University of Nebraska Press, 1984), 126. Ronda notes, "All told, the captains gathered some fourteen word lists to be sent downriver at the end of the winter. One of the lasting tragedies was that all that work was lost or misplaced after the expedition returned."

7   With one notable exception, see Robert Saindon, "The Lost Vocabularies of the Lewis and Clark Expedition," *We Proceeded On* 3, no. 3 (1977).

8   Reuben Gold Thwaites, ed., *Original Journals of the Lewis and Clark Expedition, 1804–1806* (New York: Dodd, Mead & Co., 1904), appendix.

9   Jackson, *Letters of the Lewis and Clark Expedition*, 415.

10   Ibid., 418.

11   "Reward Offered," *The Enquirer* (Richmond, Va.), May 30, 1809, 4.

12   Samuel J. Harrison (1771–1846) was a tobacco merchant who had served as a Lynchburg alderman since the Virginia town's 1805 incorporation. In 1810

Jefferson sold him two land parcels along Ivy Creek. Ruth H. Early, "Campbell Chronicles and Family Sketches," in *Embracing the History of Campbell County, Virginia, 1782–1926* (Lynchburg, Va.: J. P. Bell Company, 1927), 63–64; and James A. Bear Jr. and Lucia C. Stanton, eds., *Jefferson's Memorandum Books: Accounts, with Legal Records and Miscellany, 1767–1826* (Princeton, N.J.: Princeton University Press, 1997), 2:1254–56.

13 Barbara B. Oberg and J. Jefferson Looney, eds., *The Papers of Thomas Jefferson Digital Edition* (Charlottesville: University of Virginia Press, Rotunda, 2008).

14 Richmond, Library of Virginia, Richmond Hastings Court Suit Papers 1809: Box 13, BC 1007262 and Box 14, BC 1007261.

15 Bob Deans, *The River Where America Began: A Journey along the James* (Lanham, Md.: Rowman and Littlefield, 2007), 224.

16 Richmond, Library of Virginia, Richmond Hastings Court Suit Papers 1809: Box 13, BC 1007262 and Box 14, BC 1007261.

17 Jackson, *Letters of the Lewis and Clark Expedition*, 464.

18 Ibid., 463–64.

19 Ibid., 465–66.

20 Ibid.

21 Ibid., 470–72.

22 Ibid., 561–62.

23 Ibid., 611–13.

24 Ibid., 631–63.

25 Ibid., 635–36.

26 Edward G. Gray, *New World Babel: Languages and Nations in Early America* (Princeton, N.J.: Princeton University Press, 2014), 127–32.

27 Oberg and Looney, *The Papers of Thomas Jefferson*.

28 "Benjamin Smith Barton papers," B B284.d, Series II: Subject Files, Indian Materials, American Philosophical Society, Philadelphia, Pa.

Anishinaabe Ways of Knowing and Being

by Lawrence W. Gross
Ashgate Publishing Company, 2014

In the Anishinaabe oral tradition there are prophecies foretelling the cycles of time and experiences that the people will experience. Known as the Neesh-wa-swi' ish-koday-kawn', or Seven Fires, these prophecies predicted the coming of Europeans and the devastation of Anishinaabe cultural traditions that would ensue.[1] Many Anishinaabe people believe we are in the time of the Seventh Fire, an era proceeded by mass destruction of our cultural lifeways. While the Seven Fires prophesies predicted the loss of our cultural traditions and tremendous hardship, they are not cataclysmic warnings; they are teachings of endurance, hope, and renewal. The Seventh Fire is a time when a new generation of the Anishinaabe will go to the elders to relearn the traditional teachings and initiate a resurgence of the people and our culture.[2]

In *Anishinaabe Ways of Knowing and Being*, White Earth Anishinaabe author Lawrence Gross explores how the Anishinaabeg endured the devastating impacts of Euro-American colonization through maintaining traditional worldviews. Gross understands and articulates traditional worldview in an effort to build a new future for Anishinaabe people. He is committed to documenting an intellectual understanding of Anishinaabe worldview as a way of not only teaching and preserving the culture but also elevating it. Gross's detailed and complex understanding demonstrates time spent working in tribal communities and learning from language speakers and Anishinaabe elders. Building on the previous scholarship related to American Indian historical trauma and the soul wound, Gross adds to the literature by articulating a theory of "postapocalypse stress syndrome" (PASS). He asserts that the Anishinaabe today are starting to move beyond the effects of PASS by reaffirming the traditional role of silence in the culture; the quantum nature of Anishinabemowin (language), humor, storytelling, and rhetoric as oratory practice; and spiritual practice and growth.

The book seeks to address what happens to a society that has undergone an apocalyptic event like colonization whereby the effects of the apocalypse continue as part of the lived reality for survivors who "are faced with having to deal with the consequences of imposed cultural destruction" (33). Gross uses the phrase postapocalypse stress syndrome to describe the "resulting personal trauma, social dysfunction, and crisis in worldview" (33). Gross argues that American Indians have experienced an apocalypse as the "lifeway of a culture has come to an end. . . . The situation with the culture has changed so much that the previous way of life can never be reconstituted as it once existed. No matter how much Native Americans wish to return to life the way it was before . . . that is not going to happen. The end of their world is final" (33–34). The author makes the interesting distinction that while the American Indian world has ended, the worldview continues. He describes seventeen personal and institutional characteristics that manifest in the postapocalypse including abandonment of productive employment, hopelessness, and multiple forms of abuse. Gross's theory is critical as it describes the impact of the apocalypse not only on individuals and family but on the entire social order, including the weakening or collapse of social and cultural institutions that "would normally help people recover from societal wide trauma" (36). However, Gross offers hope for American Indian people today who are rebuilding new lifeways for their communities.

Gross's experience of Mahayana Buddhism is reflected throughout the book particularly in his observation of the use of silence among Anishinaabe people. According to Gross, long periods of silence as practiced by the Anishinaabe foster connection with the natural world, facilitate an understanding of one's own nature, and open one's heart and mind to the world. The author also provides a compelling discussion on the role of humor in Anishinaabe culture and the cultural importance of learning from pain. The embedded cultural practices of silence and humor assist in moving the people beyond the effects of PASS. Gross's chapters on the comic vision and comic mind of the Anishinaabe make an important contribution to the literature. For Gross, Anishinaabe humor is not a mere concept but a lived practice as readers will find humor interwoven throughout the book often in the most unexpected places. At the university, my colleagues regularly ask me for scholarship on American Indian humor in order to help students more fully understand Native books and films, as well as teachings from oral scholars. I am anxious to share these chapters with my colleagues.

The book is well written, and Anishinaabe readers outside of the academy will benefit from it particularly where Gross adds to our understanding of spiritual growth and how to live Bimaadiziwin (the good life) in the postapocalypse era. Here readers are reminded about the importance of fasting and dreaming as essential for our continued survival as a people. Yet, the book is written primarily for an academic audience. In particular, Gross's chapter on the quantum nature of Anishinaabemowin (language) is difficult to follow without a firm grasp of both Anishinaabemowin linguistics *and* quantum physics. Gross explains that Anishinaabe people live in both the quantum and Newtonian worlds. Anishinaabemowin is a verb-based language, in which the world is in a constant state of flux and "nothing is dead or inert. All things are alive" (105). Gross builds on previous scholarship by authors writing about modern physics and American Indian world-views. Readers may be drawn to this chapter given the success of recent books and films that sparked a popular culture interest in quantum mechanics. Readers should not reject or ignore Gross's contribution simply because it is tough to get through. The late physicist Richard P. Feynman encourages us not to turn away from quantum mechanics because it is difficult:

> What I am going to tell you about is what we teach our physics students in the third or fourth year of graduate school—and you think I'm going to explain it to you so you can understand it? No, you're not going to be able to understand it. Why, then, am I going to bother you with all this? Why are you going to sit here all this time, when you won't be able to understand what I am going to say? It is my task to convince you *not* to turn away because you don't understand it. You see, my physics students don't understand it either. That is because *I* don't understand it. Nobody does.[3]

While Gross does not clearly articulate the relationship between Anishinaabemowin, quantum mechanics, and healing from PASS, he does convince readers that these are related and important connections that warrant further examination.

The greatest strength of this book is that it contributes to the intellectual traditions of Anishinaabe written and oral scholarship. We might consider it Seventh Fire scholarship. Gross continues on the path of illumination and understanding paved by previous academic and oral scholars in the field. He builds on the work of many scholars who came before him and meets a cultural responsibility to move forward down the path of remembering the traditional teachings.

In Anishinaabe worldview, there is balance in all things. In other words, nothing in life is entirely positive and most things contain some weakness or drawback. It is law of the Anishinaabe universe that there must be gwaashkwadiziniiwin (balance and harmony) in all things. Given this, we can expect to find some problems with Gross's *Anishinaabe Ways of Knowing and Being*. To begin, Gross openly admits to hating the Green Bay Packers. However, this is an issue that should be settled outside of the academic arena. Interestingly, this statement does provide evidence that not all Anishinaabe agree with one another today. This is precisely where potential challenges to the book lie. Anishinaabe readers will likely disagree with Gross on some of his foundational arguments like the opening assertion about PASS that the Anishinaabe world has come to an end and only the worldview survives. I can hear some Anishinaabe people asserting that our worldview is inseparable from our world and that elements of both have remained, although changed, throughout the eras. It is here where the wisdom of our elders and perhaps even quantum physics will help us see these interrelationships. We can expect Lawrence Gross to continue learning from his elders and to share his understandings with us in future works. *Anishinaabe Ways of Knowing and Being* reads like the first of more books to come from this author as he continues to develop his understandings and insights so that Anishinaabe worldview will thrive.

AUTHOR BIOGRAPHY

Lisa M. Poupart is a member of the Lac Du Flambeau Band of Lake Superior Anishinaabeg. She chairs the University of Wisconsin–Green Bay First Nations Studies Program and codirects the Education Center for First Nations Studies. She is coauthor of *Connective Pedagogy: Elder Epistemology, Oral Tradition, and Community* (2013).

NOTES

1　It is clear that Gross did not expect an Anishinaabequay living less than a mile from Green Bay's Lambeau Field to diligently read his endnotes and review his book. Edward Benton-Benai, *The Mishomis Book: The Voice of the Ojibway* (Hayward, Wis.: Indian Country Communications Inc., 1988), 89–93.

2　Ibid., 188, 92–93.

3　Richard P. Feynman, *QED: The Strange Theory of Light and Matter* (Princeton, N.J.: Princeton University Press, 2006), 6.

REVIEW ESSAY *by David Martínez*

Theorizing Native Studies

edited by Audra Simpson and Andrea Smith
Duke University Press, 2014

One way of assessing the deliberate turn toward theory that the editors of *Theorizing Native Studies* advocate is to look at it within the context of Indian–white relations, in particular the Indian relation to settler-colonial education. According to eighteenth-century legend, some Haudenosaunee were "brought up" at one of the colleges in the Virginia colony, only to be regarded as completely "useless" by their people back home. Since then, indigenous communities have gone through generations of westward expansion, complete with reservations, assimilation policies (the most notorious part of which were boarding schools), urbanization, termination, relocation, and the confluence of restless Native youth and the Red Power Movement. Educationally, the latter resulted in the appearance of

American Indian/Native American studies programs at various college campuses from Minnesota to California. Now, forty-five years after AIS/NAS scholars firmly established an indigenous presence in "the academy," there is a call for "an explicit turn toward theory" on behalf of our collective intellectual and political interests.

Taken altogether, the theoretical discourses initiated in Simpson and Smith's anthology—which consists of ten essays, written by ten scholars, in ten different fields—represent the current stage of indigenous peoples' contentious history with settler-colonial theoretical systems, in which indigenous peoples have long been on the critical end of Western notions of history, evolution, religion, culture, race, and politics. With regard to which, the question arises: Is more theory the answer to the biases of non-indigenous theories and epistemologies? According to the editors: "The works in this collection share a political commitment to Native communities beyond representation within the academy. This book also affirms that Native studies is capable of developing its own analytic and methodological frameworks outside those determined by traditional disciplines or the Western academy" (22). Or, as one of the editors told me in a personal comment: "You better have your theories ready because the settlers are going to have their theories about you!" Fight fire with fire, as the old saying goes. With the latter objective in mind, the editors and their contributors were nonetheless faced with a fundamental choice: Either develop theories out of the indigenous experience, complete with their own languages and discursive styles (which will vary across peoples and places), or rely on the Western, albeit subversive, theories from the dominant settler-colonial traditions (e.g., Marx and Foucault). Mostly, what one reads in the essays assembled here is a mix of dead white male critiques of Western civilization and an array of scholars mimicking the kind of obtuse, jargon-permeated analyses that became commonplace during the rise of late twentieth-century postmodernism.

At the same time, there are moments of genuine insight into the indigenous condition, if you will, as it endures under the economic and political oppression of settler-colonial capitalist states. In this regard, Glenn Couthard's essay on the Denendeh is especially compelling, in particular the "Brief History" and "That Is Not Our Way" sections, which recount the Denendeh's epic struggle against the Canadian federal government. Also on First Nations–Canada relations, and equally compelling, is Robert Nichols analysis of "Compulsory Enfranchisement and the Gradual Civilization of the Michel Nation" in his "Contract and Usurpation" essay. If anything, *Theorizing Native Studies* makes the point that the nefarious and harmful effects of colonialism are complex, difficult to diagnose, and just as problematic to eradicate. With respect to this, Andrea Smith's essay on ethnographic entrapment and settler self-reflexivity is abundantly thought provoking. In the "Self-Confessing

Subject" section, Smith recounts a scenario from her experience with "antiracist organizing projects," in which participants confessed and earned forgiveness for their privileges as whites, males, or heterosexuals. However, one "of the reasons why there was little critique of this practice is that it bestowed cultural capital to those who seemed to be 'most oppressed'" (215). As a result, those with the least privilege in this context were the most admired. "Consequently, people aspired to be oppressed," which ironically generated an agenda that reinforced the oppressor–oppressed relationship they were supposedly interested in dismantling (216).

As one might expect, the parts of this book that live with the reader the longest are those instances when the voices of the indigenous communities shine through, providing a poignant reminder of what is most important in the work we are doing as indigenous teachers, activists, and scholars. In this regard, the brief but moving essays by Dian Million and Teresia Teaiwa stand out, as does Couthard's account of George Blondin, which includes a story that the Denendeh leader recounts about him and his brother hunting a moose. The volume concludes with Vera B. Palmer's moving but critical reflections on the life and canonization of Kateri Tekakwitha, a young Mohawk whose "sainthood" was the product of the brutalities of seventeenth-century British colonialism.

As for the specifically theoretical aspects of this volume, while all the contributors demonstrate a respect and concern for indigenous people, it is not always clear what the practical value of the theorizing is to the daily and very real lives of indigenous communities. Sometimes, the analysis has a clear and present danger in mind, such as the urgent work that Scott Lauria Morgensen is doing on the AIDS pandemic and how organizing efforts have marginalized the indigenous LGBTQ community, not to mention indigenous peoples in general. At other times, the theorizing appears to be an end in itself, in which "end in itself" means not having much value outside of the academy. As such, there are parts of this volume, including entire essays, that are simply unreadable. However, by "unreadable" I do not mean incomprehensible, but rather written with a style that obliges the reader to put more effort into parsing the ideas than into acting upon them. Then, again, expecting scholars to write without obfuscating language is frequently like expecting attorneys to forego legalese.

Speaking of mainstream institutions like the legal profession, the academy, complete with a range of programs and disciplines—of which AIS/NAS is among them—is also an institution. And institutions tend to be self-contained, resistant to change, as well as sustaining their own dialect, which may or may not be accessible to outsiders, such as our families and communities. For scholars working on indigenous issues, trying to bridge the gap between creating critiques that will have a positive impact on academic disciplines—be it the humanities, social sciences, or health—and creating discourses that indigenous people can understand and appreciate as meaningful to them is a conundrum. In the concluding section of his essay, Nichols observes: "If I am correct in suggesting that the settler contract is best understood as introducing a relationship of usurpation through practices of universal assimilation, then I hope minimally to have contributed to the richness of the theoretical vocabulary available to Native studies. However, we might aspire to more than this. The task here is to demonstrate the implication of our models of theorizing within settler colonialism, not merely to develop more sophisticated tools of analysis, which may be applied to Native studies as data" (115). What remains unclear is what is meant by "more than this."

In a history extending from Samson Occom to Vine Deloria Jr., American Indian activist-intellectuals worked outside of the academy. It is only very recently in our collective history that indigenous communities have seen the appearance of academics, beginning with D'Arcy McNickle, who founded the anthropology department at the University of Saskatchewan in 1965. In which case, the phenomenon of the indigenous professor is relatively recent. Indigenous college students, on the other hand, have constituted an adaptive tradition that goes back to the founding of institutions like Dartmouth College. Furthermore, the American Indian student body has grown substantially in years since World War II, justifying the support of AIS/NAS degree-conferring programs, in addition to scholarships, student support services, and student organizations. In turn, one can say that Simpson and Smith's book is reflective of the growth of the indigenous academic community, in particular its professoriate.

In the end, the value of *Theorizing Native Studies* is premised on accepting the colonial institution of higher education as a permanent part of our lives, complete with academic journals and conferences, grants and fellowships, and tenure and promotion. I emphasize these things to make the point that the true audience for this volume is the one that attends annual meetings of the Native American and Indigenous Studies Association—not the people back on the rez or in the cities struggling to survive. As Simpson and Smith excitedly recall in their acknowledgements: "Our panel grew from an imagined five members in total to an actuality of four panels (and more than twenty papers) . . . at the 2008 Native American and Indigenous Studies Association. . . . We then assembled another panel for the American Studies Association [2009] meeting . . . with other contributors, who also spoke of the centrality of theory and critique to the work that they do. . . . In 2010 we edited papers from those who could contribute to a book, and then we convened a workshop at Columbia University that allowed for a close reading of these texts by participants, invited discussants from

the broader Columbia community, and had a day of exceptional conversations" (vii–viii). In light of which, as an indigenous scholar, when
the editors advocate for a deliberate turn to theory, you have to ask
yourself, "If I do that, then who am I turning my back on?"

AUTHOR BIOGRAPHY

David Martínez (Gila River Pima) is associate professor of American
Indian studies at Arizona State University. He is author of *Dakota
Philosopher: Charles Eastman and American Indian Thought* (2009) and editor
of *The American Indian Intellectual Tradition: An Anthology of Writings from
1772 to 1972* (2011).

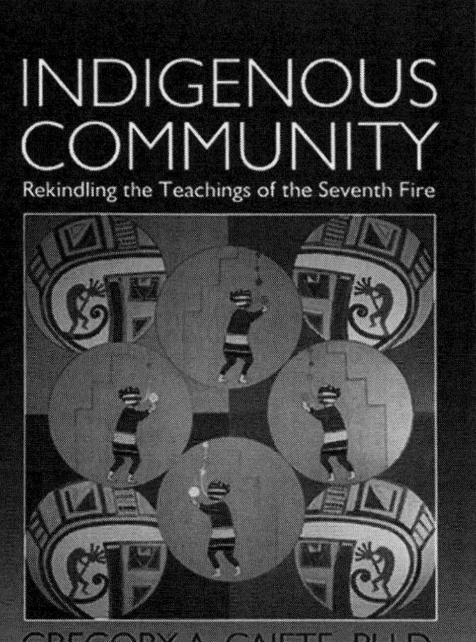

New from Living Justice Press

INDIGENOUS COMMUNITY:

Rekindling the Teachings of the Seventh Fire

by Gregory A. Cajete, Ph.D.

In his new book, Dr. Cajete examines the core concept of Indigenous teaching and learning, namely:

Community is both the medium and *the message.*

ISBN 978-1-937141-17-2
Softcover, 272 pp., indexed, $27.95

Also from Living Justice Press
Circle Forward: Building a Restorative School Community
by Carolyn Boyes-Watson and Kay Pranis
Over 100 lesson plans and ideas for using Circles in schools
Softcover, 456 pp., $60.00

order from **Living Justice Press**

livingjusticepress.org • 651.695.1008 • ljpress@aol.com

Voices from the Oceti Sakowin Oyate

From the River's Edge
By Elizabeth Cook-Lynn

Softcover, 148 pages
$20.00

He Sapa Woihanble
Black Hills Dream

Edited by Craig Howe, Lydia Whirlwind Soldier, and Lanniko L. Lee

Softcover, 229 pages, indexed, with maps
$20.00

Indigenous Nations' Rights in the Balance

An Analysis of the Declaration on the Rights of Indigenous Peoples

By Charmaine White Face, *Zumila Wobaga*

Softcover, 160 pages, indexed
$20.00

order from **Living Justice Press**

livingjusticepress.org • 651.695.1008 • ljpress@aol.com

WHEN DEMONS DANCE

A dead woman, left frozen in a rural North Dakotan ditch in January.

A lost detective, torn apart by her own frightening past, determined to find the murderer even as she struggles to unearth the truth behind her absent memories.

All fears come out to play,

when demons dance.

The newest novel from award-winning author Cara J. Swanson

Coming Halloween 2015   www.WhenDemonsDance.com